A Tribute to a
Rugby Genius

ANDREW
MEHRTENS

A Tribute to a
Rugby Genius

ANDREW
MEHRTENS

by John Matheson

HarperSports
An imprint of HarperCollinsPublishers
www.harpercollins.co.nz

IN THE BEGINNING…

THAT Andrew Mehrtens was able to rebuild his standing with the New Zealand rugby nation says much about the boy who would one day be King. Missing vital drop goal attempts in the 1995 World Cup final – ultimately lost to South Africa – is something mere mortals are not supposed to recover from.

After all, New Zealand sport is littered with reputations lost after one moment of failure on sport's unforgiving stages. Silver Fern Donna Loffegan has never been forgiven for missing an uncontested shot seconds before Sharelle McMahon landed a last second goal to deliver World Championship gold to Australia's netballers. And Otago's David Latta is always thought of in the deep south as the man who cost the Otago team Ranfurly Shield victory before they remember any of his other 160 games for the province. And Jeff Wilson, the one-time All Blacks test try, scoring record holder, will never shake the video coverage of Australian halfback George Gregan coming out of nowhere to dislodge the ball while 'Goldie' was midair and about to touch down for a famous come-from-behind victory at the Sydney Football Stadium in 1994. And how about Michael Campbell, who at the 1995 British Open produced a miraculous third-round 65 at St Andrews to lead all the big names with one round to play at golf's premier event. After stumbling in difficult conditions on the final day he could manage only third. Internationally golf's Greg Norman became a kind of tragic hero when he blew his huge lead to Nick Faldo in the last round of the Masters while Germany's Bernhard Langer once blew a simple putt that cost Europe a Ryder Cup… the list goes on.

SOME put Mehrtens' ability to overcome the disappointment of Ellis Park down to the power of youth. He was only 22 years old at the time and in his first year as an All Black. But to credit it just the fearlessness that comes with youth would be paying a disservice to Mehrtens. Those closest to him at the time know the toll missing vital kicks in the World Cup final took on him. His mother, Sandra Mehrtens, said he had taken the World Cup loss hard – blaming himself for the defeat and in particular his failed dropkick four minutes before fulltime. "He feels he has let down people like Mike Brewer and Graeme Bachop, who are retiring never having won the World Cup," she said.

His coach of the day, Laurie Mains, is in no doubt about Mehrtens' ability to overcome the goings-on at Ellis Park. "I always knew we had a very intelligent individual here in Andrew," he said in 2007. "Not just someone who had been brought up with rugby and knew the game very well. But someone who because of his supreme level of intelligence could work things out very quickly. If something wasn't working he could think on his feet in a high pressure situation and change tactics. It was no surprise that he bounced back. Because he could apply that ability to think on his feet in rugby, to life situations. He was a confident young man, with lots of ability. He knew the ability he had, so why wouldn't he bounce back? That's the difference between arrogance and self-belief and confidence. He believed in himself. He matured into a test player of world quality during 1995. It was a remarkable development that he showed. The kid was, and I don't say this lightly, a genius. The truth is, he was always going to bounce back."

Laurie Mains was worried. It was the end of the 1994 All Blacks season and from the outside looking in, things within the national set up looked healthy. The All Blacks had recovered from a 0-2 series loss to the French to defeat the touring South Africans 2-0 before drawing the last test at Auckland 18-18. That game was followed by the infamous test against the Wallabies in Sydney where George Gregan's last minute tackle on Jeff Wilson ensured an unlikely victory against the New Zealanders.

Despite the loss All Blacks supporters were upbeat with a World Cup set to follow in 1995. Jonah Lomu – while not a success against the French – had been introduced to test match rugby, Frank Bunce and Walter Little were still the best one-two punch in world rugby, Graeme Bachop reigned supreme in the global halfback wars and the likes of Zinzan Brooke, Michael Jones, Mike Brewer, Ian Jones, Robin Brooke, Olo Brown, Richard Loe and skipper Sean Fitzpatrick ensured Mains had a forward pack that was feared the world over.

But something was amiss with this All Blacks side. When the final whistle went in Sydney in August, 1994, the World Cup in South Africa was only nine months away. The only match between then and now would be a seemingly meaningless test against minnows Canada a month out from the tournament's kick-off. This was a problem because what Mains and his fellow selector Earl Kirton knew was that the All Blacks were missing one key ingredient. They had their general (read: Fitzpatrick), lieutenants (read: Bunce, Zinzan Brooke and Brewer), superstar (read: Wilson) and hatchet man (read: Loe). But what they didn't have was their pivot – the first five who would guide the black machine around the park with authority.

Since the retirement of iconic Grant Fox in 1993 Marc Ellis, Simon Mannix and Stephen Bachop had shared the No 10 jersey in eight tests. Injures had limited Ellis after he played against Scotland and England on the Northern Hemisphere tour in 1993 allowing Bachop to dominate the jersey after a solitary test was given to Mannix in the first game of the unsuccessful French series.

"The whole of our tenure was working towards getting the right mix of players in the All Blacks team to be able to play a particular style of rugby," Mains said. "We'd used Grant Fox early on knowing that he wouldn't go through to the World Cup so as his

"I didn't have to run the backline because there was so much feedback. I never questioned anything. They'd say, 'Let's do such and such.' And I'd say, 'Yep, beauty, let's do it!'"

understudies we had players like Bachop, Mannix and Ellis. Apart from Ellis – who, because of injury was never able to give the position a real go – the other players had shown they didn't really have the mental toughness required for test match football. They struggled to produce their best rugby at the highest level so we were definitely on the lookout and a little bit worried about the position."

Going into the 1994 National Provincial Championship there were three other contenders – Southland's Simon Culhane, North Harbour's Warren Burton and Canterbury's Andrew Mehrtens. Mains and Kirton spread themselves across the country to ensure they watched the trio as often as possible. It became clear quickly that the 21 year old Cantabrian was, in Mains' words, "a bit special." His first two NPC games of the season garnered a conversion and three penalties against North Harbour and three conversions and a dropped goal against King Country.

Mains was interested quickly in Mehrtens and while the country's media hacks took a little longer to 'click', that all changed a week later in Hamilton.

Until Vance Stewart took his team to Rugby Park that September afternoon most of the interest in the skinny kid from Christchurch had focused on his pedigree. Genuine rugby followers knew him from his time in the in the national under-19s against Australia in 1992 – a side which also included later Crusaders or All Black teammates Adrian Cashmore, Norman Berryman, Milton Going, Tabai Matson, Justin Marshall and Taine Randell. Before then he didn't win recognition as a schoolboy player but in 1991 he began making his mark in Canterbury in a South Island under-18 tournament that also featured Matson, Marshall and Jeff Wilson. When he turned up the next year at the trials for the national under-19s he was dubbed 'the skinny white kid'.

"I was the odd one out," he told *NZ Rugby Monthly*. "All the graduates for the New Zealand schools team knew each other, but I didn't know anyone apart from Tabai, although I remembered Justin from the previous year. He had slipped through the schools net too. Somehow I made the New Zealand team, which I'm sure was as big a surprise to all the other trialists as it was to me."

Stewart remembers it differently. "Andrew may not have had the size but he stood out because of his quickness off the mark and his tactical sense. He had the ability to work the blindside and suddenly switch the attack if that wasn't working."

In his senior debut for High School Old Boys in 1992 he scored all 15 points in the defeat of Sydenham while his first two games for Canterbury netted 45 points. His debut was against Mid-Canterbury at Ashburton. Not only did he convert ten of the team's tries but his first three touches led to tries. "I guess because I was the new boy everyone held off me so I just kept running. It was like unopposed training!"

His big break came when Canterbury's first-five and goal-kicker Greg Coffey decided to retire after the 1993 season. Mehrtens was in Italy playing for the second division club Calvisano when Stewart contacted him and asked him to return to Christchurch.

But his 'roots' were what most newshounds of the day preferred to zero in on. Mehrtens' grandfather George had played for Canterbury in the 1920s as a fullback and was an All Black in unofficial games against New South Wales in 1928. His father Terry, also a first five, represented Canterbury between 1964 and 1976 and was a New Zealand under-23 player in 1965

against the Springboks and again in 1967. Terry and his wife Sandra headed for South Africa to visit game reserves. A couple of schoolteachers, they were planning to spend one year in the Republic but they ended up staying four. Terry went on to play for Natal and played against the touring 1970 All Blacks. And because of their extended stay it meant Andrew Philip Mehrtens would be born in Durban in 1973.

Their son demonstrated an exceptional kicking prowess from a young age. Terry recalls his two year old kicking a brown plastic ball over the schoolhouse fence. "I'd come home from a day's school teaching and all Andrew would want to do was go outside and kick the ball!"

It all made good copy for news editors up-and-down the country. But by 4.30pm on September 3, 1994, Mehrtens had claimed control of his own story – and the Ranfurly Shield. Tries by wing Paula Bale, fullback Simon Forrest and skipper and flanker Mike Brewer were all converted by Mehrtens who added a vital penalty to secure a famous 29-26 win. Two weeks later in Canterbury's first defense Mehrtens' star continued to rise. Against a strong Counties side Mehrtens was sublime as he scored two tries, kicked two conversions, landed four penalties and dropped two goals in the 42-16 romp.

Mains – desperate to settle on his first-five for the following year's World Cup had an inkling he'd found his man as he watched on from the stands in Christchurch. "Andrew Mehrtens stood up for Canterbury as a player who was a wonderful kicker – both in terms of field position and at goal. He became a serious possibility for us. At the end of the 1994 season, before we decided to put him into the World Cup training squad, I spoke to Mike Brewer who I trusted. I asked him about Andrew's ability and whether he had the mental toughness to be able to handle it. I wanted to know if it would be putting too much pressure on the young man to expect him to be ready to play in a World Cup eight or nine months later.

Mike's answer was, 'Yes, he has the ability, and he has the mental toughness and it would be up to you to teach him to be a test player in time', which was a bit of a challenge from Brewer to me, which he was inclined to do. So, we made the decision to bring him in and really put the time into him.

"When Brewer talks of 'making him a test player' he means there are significant differences between playing NPC or Ranfurly Shield rugby and test rugby. It's about having the discipline, it's about having time to do what you want to do. The further up the scale you go in terms of the quality of rugby you are playing, the less time you have. That's part of the pressure. We needed to know if he had the ability to step up to the next level. It's only when you work with them, as well as watch them in the big games, then you can make an accurate judgment. So, I found it useful to talk to Brewer because the relationship between No 8s and the first-five is important. He was of the opinion that Andrew could and would do what he was told to do. Brewer knew that I was a coach that demanded teams play to a pattern and he also, as we had observed, believed it was clear that Andrew had the ability to be an exciting attacking player as well.

"And that game against Counties was significant because what we got out of that game was that this kid – when we talk about whether a player has the ability to step up to the next level – stepped up from normal NPC rugby to winning a Ranfurly Shield to defending it with some quite brilliant play. That game was a perfect example of a player being able to rise to the occasion and step up to the plate in a tough game. They're the sort of players that make potentially world class players."

The Counties challenge also, for the first time on a national scale, illustrated the remarkable personality that is Andrew Mehrtens. During an injury break in the second half, the crowd in high spirits, broke into a Mexican wave. Down on the field, Mehrtens joined in. The Canterbury coach missed it at the time but the match video told the story.

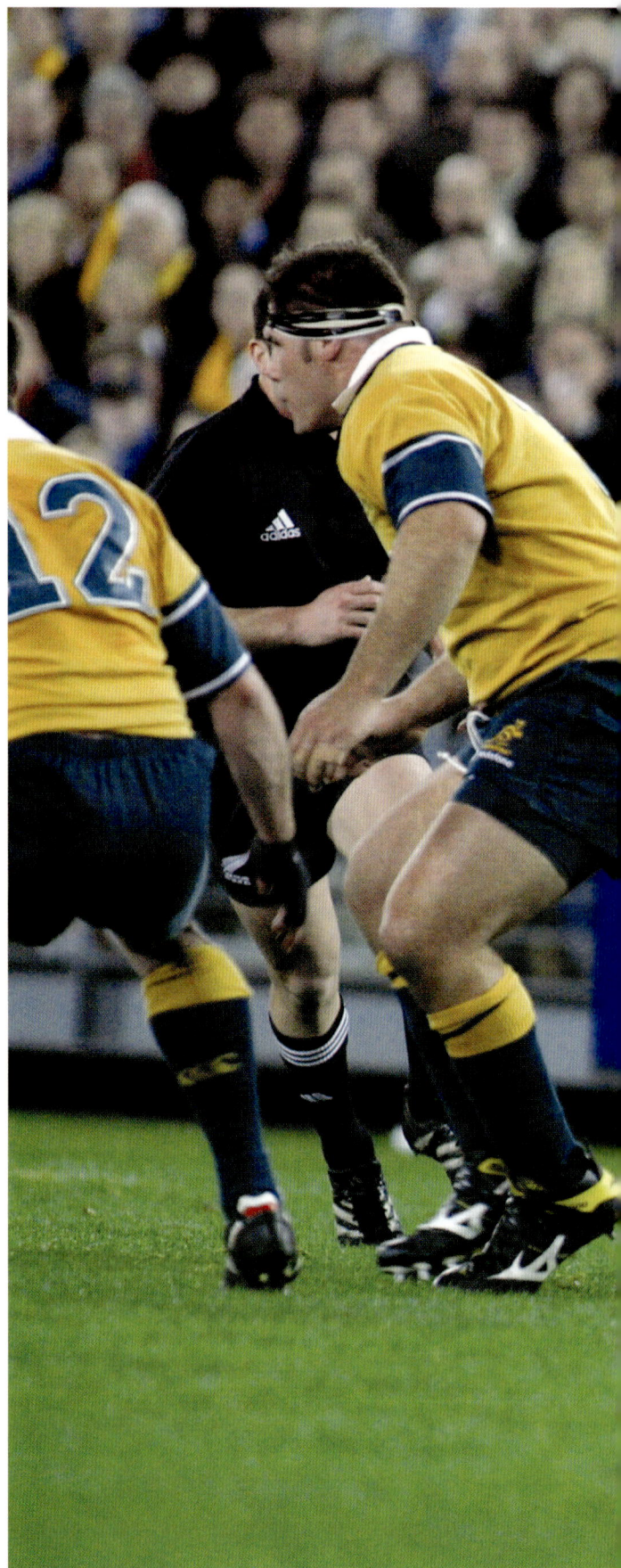

"It was so typical of him," Stewart said. "He has this amazing capacity to switch off from the serious stuff and enjoy himself. What other player would do a Mexican wave in the middle of a shield game?"

Stewart says that because of Mehrtens' effervescent personality and impish humour, people can be misled into believing he doesn't take the game seriously. "But Andrew takes every game seriously and gets very nervous beforehand. Things like doing the Mexican wave are his way of relaxing on the field."

If Mains needed confirmation it would come two weeks later when Otago challenged for the Shield. Gordon Hunter's team were on a march. Since an opening round NPC defeat to Counties they'd dispatched Waikato, Taranaki, Wellington and King Country. Locked in the middle was a 30-46 loss to Auckland but that was a result put down to referee Colin Hawke more than any inadequacies on the part of Otago. That Hawke would have the whistle for the Shield challenge had some in the South nervous but the team itself were largely unconcerned. The province had lost the Shield to Taranaki in 1957 and had failed to win it back in 13 subsequent attempts. But this time round, they thought, the jinx would finally end.

They had every right to feel confident. All Blacks John Timu, Jeff Wilson, Marc Ellis, Stephen Bachop, Jamie Joseph and Aaron Pene where joined by soon-to-be international Josh Kronfeld and should-have-been All Black John Leslie. Provincial stars like Paul Cooke and skipper and hooker David Latta added depth and belief to the Otago team.

And by the 79th minute the rugby nation were also believers as Otago led 20-19. As the forward packs battled for the ball just inside the Otago 22, Latta, inexplicably, got himself offside and Hawke duly awarded the penalty. Up stepped Mehrtens and, cool as you like, the 21-year-old slotted home the penalty goal and the Ranfurly Shield was locked away in the Canterbury trophy cabinet until the following season.

It was utter despair for Otago, for popular captain David Latta, who was the offside offender, and for the horde of Otago supporters who traveled north believing the shield was going to return to Dunedin. Canterbury's two-point win typified the usual close contests between the top two provinces in the South Island in the NPC. Four of the last eight games had been decided by that margin. It was estimated that 10,000 Otago supporters were among the 40,000 which crammed into the park. A sea of blue-and-gold banners and scarves almost obscured the embankment when Otago scored in the fifth minute. Flanker Jamie Joseph drove hard and low for the line and was helped across by fellow flanker Josh Kronfeld and prop Nick Moore. Jeff Wilson kicked the conversion from almost in front.

Canterbury, however, answered in the 13th minute, wing Paula Bale scoring a superb try after Canterbury had attacked down both flanks. Back came Otago, first five-eighths Stephen Bachop chipping ahead and skillfully retrieving his own bouncing kick. A Wilson penalty goal in the 21st minute had Otago ahead, 15-5, but Bale's second try six minutes from half time was vital. Angus Gardiner was the catalyst, grabbing an up-and-under in the face of Otago fullback John Timu and setting up the ruck. Canterbury raked back the ball and quick distribution through several hands resulted in Bale scoring wide out. After playing into the wind, Canterbury would have been pleased to be only five points in deficit at the break, but there was concern five minutes into the second half when Otago scored a brilliant try.

Timu led the break out inside his own 22m and captain David Latta twice handled as did Wilson before 'The Bear', Stu Forster, finished off. Wilson missed the conversion. He kicked only two from six, but was unlucky in that two bounced the wrong way off an upright.

Otago then went off the boil. Mehrtens chipped away at the lead with penalty goals in the 48th, 65th, and 70th minutes to have Canterbury down, 19-20. The crowd was in an uproar for the final few minutes.

Canterbury attacked, Otago defended stoutly, but then Latta burst around a ruck and South Canterbury referee Hawke caught him offside. Mehrtens was faced with a bread-and-butter kick for him, only 20m out. The pressure was immense, however, but the kick flew true and Canterbury had another shield hero.

Said Hunter about Mehrtens' kick: "That's all about life. My job on that day with regards to preparing and helping those people deal with the crisis was as significant as probably any duty I've done in the police. If you can imagine dealing with perhaps 30 people whose fathers had all died at the same time, that's what it was like afterwards. With everyone else in the room bawling, I couldn't really afford to bloody lose it myself. I would have learnt far more that day than Vance Stewart ever did in dealing with people, dealing with the emotions, dealing with a crisis, holding things together and then absorbing the criticism. Make no mistake there were a fair few arrows flying into my back after that disappointing performance. That was my chance to finally hold some silverware and it really felt as though it had been stolen away. But I knew we had competed very, very strongly; higher than anyone expected. Although one could sympathize that perhaps I could have felt sorry for myself, I felt proud."

Mains – a former Otago player and coach – couldn't afford to remain tied to his provincial roots that day. Instead he watched through All Blacks eyes. "You just had the feeling, sitting in the grand stand that day, that he would never miss that kick," Mains said. "It wasn't a difficult kick but you never felt like it wasn't going to go over when he addressed the ball. That's what you look for. We'd had a decade of it with Grand Fox and here we were about the get a player into the All Blacks with similar kicking skills but with more of an attacking game as well."

Once the NPC was complete Mehrtens was invited to a World Cup squad training camp in Auckland in December. Mains and Kirton deliberately put the player under real pressure at the camp and the first signs that

Mehrtens could be a real contender for the World Cup came when Mains addressed the media and said "He showed tremendous ability to adapt and produce what was expected of him." Thirteen years later Mains' expanded. "We didn't put the guys physically under pressure we put them under pressure skill wise. They went through pretty exhaustive skill testing and were given work to take away to work on any skills that were deficient. Now, what we found with Andrew was that he didn't really have any deficiencies. Even in the company of legends like Sean Fitzpatrick and Zinzan Brooke and under the gaze of Earl Kirton and myself, his kicking was pinpoint. His skills and concentration levels were outstanding. And he showed a very good demeanor. It didn't bother him that he was all of a sudden amongst the Frank Bunces' of this world. He just went about doing the things he was asked to do with a fair degree of ease."

The impression made by Mehrtens both in the NPC and at that first camp would have him instilled very quickly at the top of Mains' thinking when it came to No 10s for World Cup year. Mannix, Bachop and Ellis where no longer contenders. Burton had played himself out of contention when he went to pieces when the pressure was on in the NPC final against Auckland while Culhane was working his way towards being Mehrtens' back-up.

Said Mains: "When you compare Andrew's ability to step up in the big games it was something the other first fives hadn't been able to do. It was the same reason why we looked at Simon Culhane. He was a player playing under difficult circumstances because he wasn't in a great Southland side and yet he was stepping up. His tackling was outstanding as was his kicking game. He was a player who didn't crack under pressure. Of the two, in Andrew, we saw more of an attacking player and one that would reach greater heights than Simon. In selecting Simon we knew we were selecting him as the back-up to Andrew. So we decided to go for two new ones. It was frustrating that

"I've tried to keep away from building up a fear of going home. That's probably in the back of every team's mind here but we've tried to avoid that. There was probably more pressure on the 1991 team, because maybe they had more to lose – the Webb Ellis Cup for instance. We've tried to focus more on enjoyment of playing together and hopefully enjoy winning, rather than have that losing thing hanging over us."

we had to wait so long because ideally we would have liked everyone in place at the beginning of the 1994 season. But the obvious ones hadn't proven they'd be ideal for the World Cup.

"So we certainly felt better about where we were as a squad after that first camp because we'd seen Andrew in the closing stages of the 1994 season. Once he was within the All Blacks environment and we were able to make personality judgments ourselves, and knowledge and skill judgments as well, we were more relaxed and we were confident that we would have a more than adequate flyhalf for the World Cup. In fact, we were excited about it because the skills he had, really fitted into the game plan we wanted to use in 1995."

Another person impressed with Mehrtens was Fox. The then-record All Blacks points scorer from his 78 matches and 46 tests between 1984 and 1993 was not inclined to go out of his way to praise players but before the World Cup squad was selected he gave Mehrtens his seal of approval. He told the *Dominion*'s Lindsay Knight: "I've been impressed with him. He has an enormous amount of ability. He's got what it takes to go all the way. One of the things I admire is his performance under pressure. He functions well in those pressure situations. He's still young, he still has a lot of things to learn – you learn all the time when you're playing rugby and when you stop learning it's time to get out. Andrew's a fast learner. He's an intelligent player and works his options very well."

"But I believe he's a big game player," Fox said. Mehrtens was struggling with his kicking when Fox

ABOVE: A young Mehrtens impressed many – including the great Grant Fox.
PAGE 12: Mehrtens would grace the All Blacks jersey a total of 72 times.
PAGE 19: Mehrtens' goal kicking was always going to be important at the World Cup.

took charge of a kicking session at the All Blacks' summer camp in Taupo. "I began wondering. Then Graeme Bachop said to me, 'He needs 50,000 people watching him before he's any good!'"

After more camps, a Super 10 program and a number of extensive All Blacks trials Mehrtens' boyhood dream of wearing the All Blacks jersey became a reality when Mains named him at first five for the game against Canada. With the test being only five weeks out from the All Blacks' first World Cup pool game against Ireland, it was a virtual ticket to the greatest show on turf. But Mehrtens' understated reaction to his first test call-up said much about the man-child. "My primary concern here was really to just get through the trial. I wasn't really 100 per cent happy with the way I went," he said after he amassed 31 points in the shadow All Blacks Harlequins side's 96-25 rout of Waikato in Hamilton.

Leading up to his test debut it was clear Mains was impressed by his new charge. There were other new caps in the team – fullback Glen Osborne and Otago flanker Josh Kronfeld – but it was Mehrtens who stole the spotlight on and off the field.

In a pre-test meeting there was a picture taken of Mehrtens, hand held high in the air, as he was waiting to ask his coach a question. "One of the things I always cherished with Andrew was that he was always very polite, he had a cheekiness about him that was delightful and he never hesitated to ask questions if he didn't quite understand what you wanted or if he had a thought about the game plan or tactics," Mains said. "And he always expressed himself in a manner that was productive. In the early stages of the camps he showed a surprising depth of understanding of the game. He knew the game. He had the knowledge and the understanding of the game so it was only a matter of him stepping up in pace and doing the same things and he was one of those players that could make that step up quite easily.

"His inquisitive nature was quite refreshing. I'd had a history of players like that and I enjoyed it.

Sometimes it can be banter, even though there is a serious undertone. Mike Brewer questioned me from day one as a 19 year old when he came into the Otago team and I actually made him captain later that year. He questioned me from day one. Jamie Joseph was another one. Zinzan Brooke and Sean Fitzpatrick were the same. And it tells you something about them. I had a reputation of being a bit of a hard-arse and some players would be wary of me. But some of the players had no problem in asking me a question straight up – if something came across their minds and they wanted an answer they'd call on me to answer it. It told me more about those players – they had that mental toughness and confidence. It didn't matter who they were talking to or against, they'd have their say. And that's what you look for in top level rugby players. You don't want mentally weak people. You want people who have confidence and who are tough. And I respected players that asked intelligent and genuine questions. It was always challenging for me to make sure I had the right answers or, if I didn't have the right answers to go to other players. Andrew was one who always did it in the right manner but there was always that glint of challenge in his eye. *Have I got you this time Laurie?* I loved it. I welcomed it."

Mehrtens took every opportunity available to seek out and talk to Fox before his debut at Eden Park. And he was relishing running out as an All Black for the first time – and the nerves that went a long with it. "I like to be nervous, it helps get me to a good activity level," he said the day before the test. "I've made a conscious effort not to think too much ahead and to keep it to one thing at a time. I put too much pressure on myself in the Super 10 in thinking too much into the future and about the World Cup. All I can do is go out and do my best without worrying what repercussions that has. I have to do my best for the game's sake and the team's sake and whatever happens from there will happen."

What happened was the All Blacks sprinted home 73-7 with Mehrtens scoring 28 points and so in his first test had the heady distinction of becoming the All Blacks' test record scorer on debut, beating the 26 that Fox scored against Fiji in 1987 and Allan Hewson against Australia in 1982. His tally was also a world record for a player on test debut, beating Matthew Cooper's 23 points against Ireland in 1992.

Perhaps more important than the records was how he went about collecting his record haul. Lindsay Knight, the great *Dominion* scribe, summed up Mehrtens' try, seven conversions and three penalty goals writing: "Mehrtens showed he has the ability to become a world class inside back, combining the qualities of two of New Zealand's best in the position in recent years, Grant Fox and Frano Botica. He punted for position and the corners with Fox-like precision and in scampering on the double-round outside left wing Jeff Wilson for a try, showed some of Botica's mercurial attacking qualities."

Another who was impressed was the All Blacks second five, Walter Little. He told the press corp after the test that there was no need for him to 'baby' the debutante. "The three of us (Little, Bunce and Mehrtens) talked a lot through the game. In fact we were always talking – it was his first test match and a big day for him. Me and Frank were the experienced guys out there to look after him, but the way he played was like a natural. He had a brilliant game. He reminded me of my days outside Frano Botica. The guy is so talented and the backline buzzed thanks to him. He's my kind of partner. Where a Grant Fox plays the percentage game, Mehrts will have a go even in a 30-70 situation. It had to be 60-40 before Foxy would try anything. They're both superboots but Mehrts has dazzling acceleration."

Mehrtens was thrilled with his instant rapport with Little and Bunce. "I didn't have to run the backline," he said, "because there was so much feedback. I never questioned anything. They'd say, 'Let's do such and such.' And I'd say, 'Yep, beauty, let's do it!'"

Mehrtens' form was so good that Mains excluded him from the final trial where Culhane and Stephen Bachop fought it out for the back-up job. Mehrtens, in the space of nine months, had won his spot in the World Cup squad. And the country's love affair with him was well and truly under way as his character oozed out of him. This was a young man whose brain was so sharp he won a scholarship for calculus while at college. He possessed a photographic memory – once he sees a phone number he never forgets it. And he was always up for a laugh. When a television reporter before the Canadian test asked him if he would ever go to league he said "No, I'm too important for the All Blacks." *Isn't that an arrogant attitude? Why do you consider you are so important?* "Because," he said, "I'm in charge of the laundry and no one else understands the system!"

IT was the best of times, it was the worst of times. It was a time when New Zealand's rugby heroes would be tested like never before. A bout of food poisoning before the World Cup final would make sure of that. This was a cruel blow to a team that had set new standards for the game that winter in 1995. Never had a team played such a relentless brand of attacking rugby. Never had a team won through to the final of the game's biggest event so emphatically. And the rugby world certainly had seen nothing like Jonah Lomu before.

The giant wing stole the headlines as the All Blacks steamrolled their opposition in group play. Ireland were dispatched 43-19 before Wales were steamrolled 34-9. In two games against strong Five Nations competition the All Blacks had scored eight tries, with Mehrtens collecting 34 points thanks to five conversions and eight penalties.

"He was thriving," says Laurie Mains. "He was a good tourist. He never appeared to have off days in

terms of his moods. He was young and respectful to the senior players but contributed usefully. He was an outgoing personality with a real cheek. Right through the time I had him he continued to be like that – he could always crack a smile and a joke without ever being disrespectful to the people around him. There was never any sign of arrogance from him. And on the park he was superb. The third pool game, against Japan, could have an ideal game for a young player to get some confidence. But he didn't need the game. His play was at a level where I don't ever remember having to talk to him about specific things that he needed to sharpen up on. When we talked, we'd just talk tactics. So he had his week off and turned out against Scotland in the quarterfinals and played quite brilliant rugby. He's naturally a confident guy and if the people around him were doing a good job – as they were – he just continued to grow."

His mature and relaxed approach was confirmed when he sat down with *Evening Posts'* David Ogilvie the night before the Scotland test. "I've been lucky to play against different opponents each time, so everything's new and exciting. We're all looking forward to getting into the quarters. There's a wee bit more riding on it because, if you lose, you're out completely. So that makes it more pressure," he told Ogilvie. "I don't [feel], or haven't felt yet, overwhelming pressure but I enjoy the thrill and excitement of it. I'm looking forward to it and I'm sure everyone else is as well. I don't know much

ABOVE: Jonah Lomu was the out and out star of the 1995 World Cup.
FOLLOWING PAGES: Mehrtens was all concentration when lining up a kick.

about Scotland because I haven't been around much. And that's probably a good thing because you go in there with no expectations, other than that you will be going into a very hard game. I've tried to keep away from building up a fear of going home. That's probably in the back of every team's mind here but we've tried to avoid that. There was probably more pressure on the 1991 team, because maybe they had more to lose – the Webb Ellis Cup for instance. We've tried to focus more on enjoyment of playing together and hopefully enjoy winning, rather than have that losing thing hanging over us.

"I think it's a wee bit easier for some of us in the team – the younger ones. We are seen as new, younger guys and there's almost a feeling that if we do really stuff up badly, it will all get put down to youth and inexperience. There's also the point that other teams haven't seen us before, and guys say back home that the first year of your provincial rugby is your easiest and the second your hardest, because people have watched you and analysed you. So maybe we're still at the honeymoon stage at the moment."

With Scotland beaten 48-30 – with Mehrtens' scoring a try (a 65m dash down the sideline) and kicking six conversions and two penalties for a haul of 23 points – the honeymoon continued through to the semifinal against England. Certainly England's highly rated first five Rod Andrew has been impressed by the Cantabrian. "I rate him very highly in all areas. His goal kicking is obviously a key area. Some of his kicking out of hand with both feet has been outstanding, his distribution, the number of tries New Zealand has scored… he looks to me to have become a pretty key part of the New Zealand side very quickly. Clearly the New Zealanders have brought a very open style to the World Cup, which does put a bit more pressure on the flyhalf to maintain that. And he's been an integral part of that approach."

If Andrew was trying to lure the younger Mehrtens into a false sense of security, his teammate Will Carling blew any supposed plot by coming out the following day and lambasting the charge of the All Blacks youth brigade – Lomu, Mehrtens, Josh Kronfeld and Glen Osborne. "There are one or two younger players in there for New Zealand who haven't been tested," Carling said. "We believe that we have the side to put them under the sort of pressure that they haven't experienced yet. Someone like Lomu has been dynamic with the ball in his hands, but has anyone really had a go at him yet? I believe Tony Underwood is capable of that."

It took just three minutes for Jonah to make his point. "Jonah uses these remarks positively," Bunce told Ogilvie. "It's at your own peril if you make remarks like that to Jonah. He reads these comments, takes them in and uses them positively against his opponents."

The All Blacks had hit the ball at pace from the very start, the startled English forwards made to turn and chase. Then the ball went wide, and a wild pass was thrown past Lomu towards touch. He halted, turned, picked it up and faced foe No 1 Tony Underwood, a man who had openly voiced doubts about Lomu midweek. Wap! A paw in the face and Lomu was gone. Carling was left sprawling but managed to just upset the Lomu carriage. Staggering towards England fullback Mike Catt, Lomu ran straight over him, and reached out a big arm to score. It was the most awesome display of physical power at the World Cup.

A minute later the All Blacks were in again. Walter Little reached back, plucked the ball in and burst past Jeremy Guscott. Twenty metres further on Osborne jetted away from Carling and re-fed Little. Things got a little messed up a few metres out, but Josh Kronfeld did the cleaning up and scored. Four minutes gone and 12-0, and the England challenge had run into the side of Table Mountain.

"We really needed a good start," said Bunce. "It was intense in the changing-room and we were ready.

It doesn't help that after you do the haka you wait around for two or three minutes waiting for television, but we were so worked-up and fizzed-up we just knew it was going to happen."

Before the eighty minutes was up Lomu had added another two tries and Graeme Bachop had also touched down. Lost in the hype around Lomu was the news that Mehrtens, with 12 points, had scored the fastest 100 points in test rugby. It had taken him only five tests.

The victory was significant because the 45-29 demolition of England gave a glimpse of the future at the expense of a side which had genuinely believed it could lift the William Webb Ellis Cup. Superior in pace, skill and invention to the European champions, the All Blacks touched perfection in the opening 30 minutes. Two passages of play – neither directly involving giant wing Jonah Lomu – epitomised the New Zealand performance.

At the kick-off Mehrtens lined up his forwards to the right, then kicked to the left to give New Zealand an instant attacking platform as two England players collided going for the ball. Mains would later reveal the move had been planned six months ago. And later in the match No 8 Zinzan Brooke, who had already stunned England by drop-kicking a goal, found a perfect touch from the dummy scrum-half position, bouncing the ball over the touchline with his left foot.

It was heady stuff and predictably Mains, initially at least, had few worries going into the final. There was nothing about the All Blacks performances that needed anything more than fine-tuning. "Against England we executed the game plan we had worked on for a year. We kicked off towards the wrong side, we just wanted to do anything and everything to upset their forwards and not let them settle into a pattern. And when we needed to take them on up front we did that as well. But we did it when we chose too, not when they wanted us too. Andrew, his execution of the game plan that day was just outstanding. Creating the space for

Jonah to do the damage he did – Graeme Bachop and Andrew were brilliant at giving the ball air and doing it quickly. Things were going very well."

Mehrtens was at his cheeky best before the trick kick-off. He realised that if they didn't tell the referee, Ireland's Steve Hilditch, he might stand in the way and wreck the moment. As Colin Meads tells the story: "Mehrts decided he'd have to come with me to explain, because I might mess up the description. So I was there being all polite and good to the referee, and Mehrts takes over: 'Look ref, it'll happen suddenly, so make sure you get out of the way and don't bugger it up.' All the ref could do was go: 'Ah yes, I'll keep it in mind.' Mehrts wasn't trying to be cheeky or rude, but before a game he's so bouncy and perky, it just came out. Mehrts is one of those guys who has to be bouncy to give his best. You'd hate to see him change."

So, all was well within the All Blacks camp but… the first signs of trouble became public when this report was filed by the New Zealand Press Association. *"There was some concern in the All Black camp about the health of first five-eighths Andrew Mehrtens on the eve of the Rugby World Cup final. Mehrtens is yet another victim of the flu problem which has attacked many players and camp followers in recent weeks. He looked less than a picture of health today but it was hoped that a good night's sleep would put him back on top."*

It, of course, wasn't the flu. The All Blacks – 24 hours out of the final – were the victims of an outbreak of food poisoning. Mains would later suggest that there may have been something suspicious about the episode. Eighteen members of the 26-man squad suffered after a lunch in their hotel on Thursday. Mains claimed on New Zealand radio that the after-effects had "significantly affected" his side's performance in the final.

The side's media liaison officer Ric Salizzo said the team's management had no proof the players had been deliberately poisoned. "It certainly wasn't a virus because we all went down with it at the same time," Salizzo said. "We deliberately didn't say anything before the game and we only mentioned it afterward when people asked us about it. It's pretty hard to keep quiet in those circumstances."

Mains had told *Radio New Zealand*: "It was just an amazing sequence of events and coincidence that of our 35-man party that ate at that particular lunch venue in the hotel here, about 27 of them went down in the space of 12 hours. You can read what you like into that, but I don't think it was coincidence. We certainly have our suspicions."

Regardless of whether the All Blacks were deliberately poisoned or not the reality is ten of the starting All Black 15 were affected, including Jeff Wilson, prop Craig Dowd and Mehrtens – the three worst affected. "It was a situation which left us with a bit of chaos on Friday just not knowing who was going to play and who wasn't," Mains said. "That in itself had an effect on our mental preparation for the game. There have been no further developments, nor would there be and nor could there. The fact of the matter is we had a fair number of players who went down with food poisoning."

Lochore would later say: "No one can ever say conclusively how we became ill and in my opinion it's something that should now be forgotten. But the fact is that on the Thursday after having eaten lunch at our hotel 22 of our 35-man squad and 10 of the playing 15 became ill. Everyone was sick in varying ways. We ate in a sectioned-off part of the dining room and had a variety of foods. The only thing we had in common was coffee and tea and the milk which went into them. We deliberately kept it away from the press, who were staying in the same hotel and presumably ate in the main part of the dining room, on the Friday. We didn't want to give South Africa any sort of advantage of knowing we were off colour. When it came out after the game, we couldn't win, either, because inevitably it would look like sour grapes."

"It was a kick I would expect to land nine times out of ten.
I was terribly disappointed because that is what I was supposedly
there to do. But do I feel I lost the game? No. That was just one
moment in the one hundred minutes that made up the final.
I felt bad about it, but there were dropped passes and a host of
other mistakes that lessened our effectiveness that afternoon."

Meads says brief thought was given to shifting the game, because the All Blacks had no chance of fielding a properly fit team, but it would have been impossible because of both the match and international television arrangements. "In hindsight perhaps we should have done that," he said. "And perhaps, too, we should have said at the time we had so many sick players instead of trying to keep our state away from the opposition."

The All Blacks doctor Mike Bowen said that all of the squad appeared to be well on the Thursday. At lunch some ate hamburgers, others chickenburgers, some pasta and some sandwiches. There was no common denominator to anything consumed. The only thing in common was the coffee and tea.

"There is no proof of any outside intervention," Bowen told *The Dominion*. "Three bowel samples were tested in a Johannesburg laboratory but that proved nothing. But there still has to be significant doubts why so many people eating such a variety of food got so sick when nobody else in the hotel was affected. There was no common denominator that was what was most unusual. It's amazing to think something like this should happen on the eve of the team's biggest game when they'd been together six weeks and nothing like this had happened in the two years I'd been with the team. It all doesn't quite add up. There was no doubt it was going to have a huge impact on performance. It had a physical impact as well as a psychological one. It was a terrible situation and I was up most of the Thursday night rushing around like a flea in a fit. A number of the people needed care all night long."

Bowen said that those who were ill were affected in varying ways. Some vomited, others had diarrhea. The worst affected were Wilson and Mehrtens, who were still ill on the Friday when Bowen thought they would not be able to play the final. Though they recovered, Bowen says he has no doubts that they and others would probably not have been at their physical best for the match.

The final was lost 15-12, after extra-time. If judging the final purely on the spectacle South Africa proved that a good defence – backed up with the boot of Joel Stransky – could beat the best offence on the planet prompting leading rugby scribe Duncan Johnstone to opine "The Springboks completed a remarkable three years back in international rugby when their captain, Francois Pienaar, lifted the Webb Ellis Cup before a joyous crowd of 65,000 and an adoring country. The All Blacks completed a remarkable six weeks with nothing to show other than the tag of being the most exciting team at the tournament."

Springbok coach Kitch Christie summed it up when he said: "Defence won the game. Our tackling was unbelievable… our loose forwards, our backs. But it was a typical final. It could have gone either way."

The All Blacks performance was a confused one. They tried to run the ball out of their own 22m from the start when in previous games they had often been prepared to kick for field position. And when they did find themselves within sight of the Springbok posts, they more often than not abandoned the running game that had produced all those tries in the lead up. Mehrtens kicked two dropped goals from three attempts before the final. Against South Africa he tried the drop-kick five times and was successful just once.

Mehrtens would live to rue a miss 2min 10s from ordinary time when Ian Jones had won one of his 18 lineout takes, 15m from the Springbok line and Frank Bunce had set up the ruck just to the left of the posts. The score was 9-9, Mehrtens received good ball but pushed his kick wide and the match went into 20 minutes of overtime – the first in cup history. In the end it was left to Stransky to seal the game with a 38m dropped goal off a Zinzan Brooke mistake eight minutes from the end.

Had this been an ordinary game in ordinary circumstance it could be argued the criticism leveled at Mehrtens – who kicked three penalties to go with his one dropped goal – in the aftermath on the radio waves in New Zealand immediately after the game was justifiable. But this was no ordinary affair. The All Blacks' fate was sealed before the game by way of the food poisoning. Certainly, once the game was sent into extra-time, the game was as good as lost.

Mains is adamant he knows how history *must* judge Mehrtens when discussing that June afternoon in Johannesburg. "I would never judge Andrew on the final. He missed things that he wouldn't ordinarily miss but I would never make a judgment on that because like most of the other players he was playing under extreme difficulty. We all know that when you get a stomach upset and you are vomiting, how that can affect your mental capacity and coordination. All I had for all of those players that played that day was absolute admiration for gusting it out the way they did.

"The fact that they could still have won the game was probably an indication of not only the guts of the team but of how much better they probably were than the opposition considering most of them played at 80 per cent.

"You know, I've talked about that World Cup hundreds of times. But I have never once spoken about the drop goal. It is in my opinion very unfair for it to be raised given the state of the game and the difficulty heath-wise that the player was operating under. So I have never commented or had an opinion on it. And I want to keep it that way because I would never want anyone to think that I, in any shape or form, would be critical of Andrew for that. This is the first time I've actually mentioned it.

"We were all shattered after the loss. And the biggest part of that was that we knew that we weren't able to go out there and play the way we could have played. That was the shattering part as much as not winning. What it did was bring us a lot closer as a group of people. A loss, or not achieving something, can separate people but on this occasion it didn't because we all knew what had happened. To my knowledge, no one had any ill-feelings towards anyone else in the team. I think we all had sympathy for each other. No player on that day could have a finger pointed at him to say he'd let the All Blacks down. You just couldn't say that."

Mehrtens, in time has come to deal with the disappointment of the day. "It was a kick I would expect to land nine times out of ten. I was terribly disappointed because that is what I was supposedly there to do. But do I feel I lost the game? No. That was just one moment in the one hundred minutes that made up the final. I felt bad about it, but there were dropped passes and a host of other mistakes that lessened our effectiveness that afternoon."

Once back in New Zealand Mehrtens did what he normally did to deflect his audience, be it the media or a parliamentary reception... he turned to humour. He told them his greatest memory from South Africa was dirty washing – of course he was 'privileged' to be assigned to the All Black camp's all-important laundry committee.

"And I can tell you it was a nightmare! It's one of the jobs they hand out to the new kids. We had to look after the laundry at each hotel we stayed in. It was a very important job, you know. There were dangers – we had to make sure training gear with brand names didn't go missing. An unbelievable nightmare – some of the guys would leave their jerseys behind, they wouldn't label their socks properly... Some guys were pretty good. I can say Jeff Wilson was a real delight to launder for. Jamie Joseph would have to be one of the worst."

At parliament he said he was disappointed his choir-boy looks haven't yet landed him a role in commercials. He suggested his face could adorn the box of a laundry detergent... "I'm also a bit disappointed I haven't had any league offers yet. Not that I'd want to play league. I'd just like to be offered (it) so I can say no."

There was some seriousness though too. A month after the final the All Blacks had the small matter of two tests against Australia to play. The Bledisloe Cup was at stake and Mehrtens made sure the New Zealand public knew the players charged with winning it were as motivated as ever. He said there would be no World Cup hangover. "There's unfinished business here. I don't think anyone felt worse than anyone else after the final but we were all pretty shattered. However, we've only looked forward since then. This is a way we can make some small amends to New Zealand. The prize is the Bledisloe Cup, which Australia has and we want."

The first of the two tests was played at Eden Park and Mehrtens had opportunity to reflect on what might have been a month earlier when he landed two 40-metre dropped goals in his collection of 23 points as the All Blacks won comfortably 28-16. And a week later in Sydney the Bledisloe had been won when in a dazzling display the All Blacks reproduced a performance on a level with the showing against England at the World Cup beating Bob Dwyer's team 34-23. Bunce, Lomu, Wilson and Mehrtens all scored tries with the Cantabrian adding another nine points with his boot.

"People were watching him closely – wondering if there were any mental scares left over from the final of the World Cup," Mains said. "It was clear there weren't."

Mehrtens' first year as an All Black was now over. After winning a battle with a shoulder injury picked up in Canterbury's unsuccessful defence of the Ranfurly Shield against Auckland in September, he was selected for Mains' last tour as All Blacks coach to Italy and France. But he ruptured the anterior cruciate ligament of the right knee running in the open against Italy A at Catania. The knee had to be completely reconstructed and it would be seven months before he was back in action.

ABOVE: Laurie Mains – the first All Blacks coach to select Andrew Mehrtens.
OPPOSITE: Mehrtens in fine form.

THE HART OF
THE MATTER...

JOHN Hart was public enemy No 1. He was the first All Blacks coach to publicly blame a player for a defeat. And it didn't help his cause that the player in question was the by now extremely popular Andrew Mehrtens. It was, it could be argued, the moment when Hart lost his All Blacks public. It was, without a doubt, a moment he would never recover from.

THIS was a new era. In the aftermath of the 1995 World Cup rugby had turned professional. After a heated battle played out in back rooms of players' homes, hotel rooms and at the homes of multi-millionaires, a break-away group – the World Rugby Corporation – had failed to sneer the All Blacks away from the black jersey. To a man the players re-signed with the NZRU and the future of the game was secure. Player payments were introduced in time for the All Blacks' tour to Italy and France and a new competition featuring 12 teams from Australia, South Africa and New Zealand was formed and called the Super 12. It was exciting stuff and the man who would lead New Zealand rugby into this brave new world was John Hart.

He was the polar opposite to the man he had replaced at the helm of the All Blacks. Laurie Mains was from the South. Hart from Auckland. Mains' business deals were done in jeans and shirts with sleeves rolled up. Hart's were done in a suit – the finest money could buy. Mains had played for the All Blacks. Hart hadn't. And Mains' tenure as All Blacks coach ended with the Brooke brothers – Zinzan and Robin – carrying him off the Parc des Princes after a 37-12 win against the French in Paris. In contrast Hart's previous attempt at coaching the All Blacks – as a co-coach with Alex Wyllie in 1991 – had ended in disaster with a semifinal defeat at the hands of the Wallabies in Ireland.

Hart's appointment was popular – if you lived north of the Bombay Hills. Mains and his team had won the hearts of the country the previous year and it would take two years before Mains' shadow could be cast from Hart's All Blacks. In 1996 – Hart's first year in charge – there was little doubt that he was coaching Mains' team. The large majority of players were 'Mains' boys' while the game plan that would be instilled certainly was. There would be new caps in Hart's first year but any success – rightly or wrongly – was always going to be tainted as far as Hart was concerned because regardless of his own influences on the team,

the critics would for ever remind him that his team was the one Mains built.

Hart certainly was keen to monitor Andrew Mehrtens' recover from his brutal knee injury. He made it clear early on that Mehrtens would form a key role in his plans. Indeed, at one stage Mehrtens was even regarded as captaincy material. With a full tour of South Africa planned, a mid-week All Blacks captain was needed.

For a while some critics suggested there may also be a change of skipper for the first XV. Hart's relationship with Sean Fitzpatrick had never been close. It was only toward the end of Hart's term as Auckland's coach that Fitzpatrick became Auckland's regular hooker and when Fitzpatrick first became an All Black in 1986, he was second string hooker in Auckland. In recent years, as Fitzpatrick increasingly became an ally of Laurie Mains, there were some tart observations about Hart's man-management style, particularly in Fitzpatrick's 1994 autobiography. But there was little likelihood of a leadership change being made with the haste similar to when Mains in 1992 dismissed Gary Whetton.

Fitzpatrick would hold off any challenge from Zinzan Brooke, and Richard Loe and Frank Bunce were never real contenders for the top job either. But the four games outside the tests in Africa would offer Hart a chance to examine the potential options. His shortlist included Taranaki's Mark Allen, North Harbour's Liam Barry, Otago's Taine Randell, Anton Oliver and Mehrtens.

Mehrtens would though have little chance to impress on the field before the first test of Hart's era – against Manu Samoa at McLean Park in Napier. He would miss the entire Super 12 season as he fought back to full fitness. Instead he played a communicative role for the Canterbury Crusaders acting as a link man between the team, the media and those wanting access to the players.

"Assuming all goes well, I would like to be in contention for some invitation games in May like the

"After the World Cup final I wasn't eager to risk everything on a dropped goal. We practice moves at training all the time and hardly ever use them so I called one we'd worked at that very week. The Wallabies obviously didn't think we would go for a try. Frank Bunce put me into the gap and it was a wonderful sensation to realize I had two of the fastest players in the world – Christian Cullen and Jeff Wilson – in support. That try gave us all a huge buzz."

Harlequins against Waikato and the Centurions against Bay of Plenty," he told NZPA at the beginning of the season. "I've talked to some people about that and it does not seem too unreasonable at this stage. But any hiccups at all and I won't be risking it. I saw (Auckland surgeon Barry Tietjens) two weeks ago and he is very happy with the way things are going. Three months are nearly up, and if I get the go-ahead I'll get into touch and tennis and get everything moving laterally. I've had a couple of games of touch without getting carried away. I'm taking it cautiously. Up to now the emphasis, as well as doing weights, has been on balance because from your balance comes your confidence."

Hart – much maligned for his man-management style – made an effort to keep Mehrtens involved and despite his injury invited him to a seminar to discuss the perils and pitfalls of professional sport. The all-day Auckland seminar, involving 46 players, included advice on contract and legal obligations, financial management, rugby's judicial process, sponsor and media relations. A further sign of Hart's desire to continue to nurture Mehrtens came when he included him in the All Black players' committee alongside Sean Fitzpatrick and Ian Jones.

While Hart was planning for the future the Crusaders were cursing their luck. The franchise that would eventually go on to dominate the competition in years to come was in crisis. The first three game of the season were lost before a draw and win against Western Province and New South Wales respectively. By the time of the game against Northern Transvaal – which would also be lost – pressure was coming on coach Vance Stewart to bring Mehrtens back early. To his credit he didn't – although the sight of Mehrtens goal kicking at High School Old Boys' training at the time must have made it very tempting to take the No 10 jersey off Greg Coffey and Graeme Dempster and hand it to Mehrtens.

"It's mainly the strength of my leg that is holding me back at the moment, the knee itself is absolutely sweet," said Mehrtens at the time. "It's the other things… the match conditioning and I've lost quite a bit of muscle strength in my quad. But I'm getting that back quickly. I've been goal kicking for about three or four weeks although I haven't put a hell of a lot of time into it yet. That was mainly a confidence thing… to stretch my leg out with no hassles." Mehrtens had been playing touch rugby since January and running regularly but admitted at being frustrated with the wait on the sidelines. "Time has gone quickly but it's one of those situations where the closer you get, the further away it seems. If I progress, I should be well right by June (and the tests). But I'm not expecting anything, I'm just going quietly with it and we'll see how it works out."

As the loses continued to pile up for the Crusaders, Mehrtens would make a low-key return to rugby on April 17 when he turned out for High School Old Boys against Sumner in a Christchurch metro club division three match under lights. He kicked four from five penalties and missed two sideline conversions in his side's 24-22 loss. Two weeks later, after his third club game, he declined an invitation to make his Super 12 debut in the final game of the year against the Highlanders – thus avoiding any link to a miserable season which saw the Crusaders finish last with only two wins from their 11 games. Instead his reemergence on a national scene would come with a game for the New Zealand Harlequin XV against Waikato.

Grant Fox – the great All Blacks No 10 – was in no doubt that despite missing the Super 12 Hart had to invest in Mehrtens once the test season began. "He's the complete player and the one guy coach John Hart must look to this season," Fox said. "Being such a wonderfully skilled player is so important but it is his leadership skills that are also vital. He is so astute at implementing the right strategy that it's more and more apparent he must call the shots in the backline. The All Blacks have got some wonderful firepower in the backs and we need a player of Mehrtens' vision to unleash it at the right time."

Fox said Mehrtens' kicking game also made him the ideal man to wear the No 10 jersey.

"In all three areas of kicking for goal, at restart and tactical, Mehrtens has excelled and all are absolutely critical for the All Blacks." And he didn't want to contemplate an international season without the Cantabrian. "The problems will be compounded (if Mehrtens isn't fit) because he offers the total package. If he can't play then you have to look at rearranging the backline and also at other goal kickers. Too many players have been hot and cold. Simon Culhane has been ill and would take a while to come back. Carlos Spencer can be very, very good but he can have his off days. Stephen Bachop is devastating when he gets fast ball on a plate from his forwards but can struggle when that's not happening. Jamie Cameron got big raps and then was dropped. Ian Foster is a sound tradesman but perhaps he's not what's required. There's a lot to think about if Mehrtens couldn't play. If you want to play an attacking game, Carlos has got the flair to do that but other aspects of his game, like kicking, would have to be worked on. That's why I can't reiterate how important it is that Andrew makes a successful comeback."

And that's just what Mehrtens did in Hamilton as he spearheaded the Harlequins to a 52-49 win. He succeeded with only five of 11 shots at goal and in general play was also guilty of some miss-kicks. But there were also some of the superb touches he showed for the All Blacks the previous year, including one searing break that brought an early try to left wing Matthew Carrington. "We have to keep in mind this was really a festival match," Hart said afterwards. "But it was good to see some of those out with injury come through so well, especially Andrew Mehrtens. There's a way to go yet but this was an encouraging step up for him. We're a little more relaxed than what we were."

Mehrtens continued his progression towards an All Black jersey with a convincing display in a pre-season rugby match for the Air New Zealand Invitation XV against Nelson Bays at Trafalgar Park. He kicked seven

conversions and created plenty of attacking momentum as his makeshift line-up overran the home team 64-26.

A day later he was in the All Blacks trial and named in the President's XV. That his teammates included the new phenomenon Christian Cullen and established All Blacks like Jeff Wilson, Frank Bunce, Jonah Lomu, Zinzan Brooke, Josh Kronfeld, Ian Jones, Robin Brooke, Sean Fitzpatrick and Craig Dowd was a clear sign that Mehrtens was right back to where he wanted to be – although he was second guessing himself the day before the game against the Barbarians.

"The fitness isn't so great but every game gets easier," Mehrtens said. "In the Harlequins game I found myself puffing a wee bit because it was fairly hot. It's good when I play club rugby because in those games you throw the ball around a lot, it's experimenting, it's very quick and there's not much structure. I'm just pushing myself in club games but if, after that, I don't feel up to it I'll be doing a lot of work leading up to the trial – running and stuff. I'm just rapt to be playing. There's nothing like really getting out and playing, it's just the knocks and things that throw you for starters."

He need not have worried. The Presidents XV won 72-18 with Mehrtens looking sharp as he unleashed a backline that collected Wilson (3), Cullen (3), Lomu (2) and Scott McLeod (1) nine tries. Hart was happy telling the press: "If you look at the fellow's (Mehrtens) build-up that was pretty magic."

As expected Mehrtens was named in the test side for the game against Samoa. The team included two new caps – Cullen and McLeod. Like the rest of the country Mehrtens was a fan of Cullen – the Hurricanes fullback who had burst onto the scene with a phenomenal Super 12. "It's great to have a guy, and Glen Osborne was the same, who if you give him the ball doesn't have to be in a gap – he just makes something out of it." Work on Cullen to 'bring him out of his shell' was almost immediate. The extroverted Mehrtens 'interviewed' Cullen for a supposed television audience. It may never have been seen, but was a classic. Mehrtens tended to dominate, but Cullen managed to give captain Sean Fitzpatrick 'all credit' for clearing the ball from a maul for one of the President's XV's tries.

Despite suffering from a slight calf strain Mehrtens would start the first test of the Hart era – the first alongside his Canterbury teammate, halfback Justin Marshall who had debuted in Paris the year before. And the start to Hart's reign was classy – a 51-10 win with Cullen, who scored three tries, grabbing the headlines. Mehrtens too could be satisfied with his performance. He collected 16 points but it was his ability to vary his play which proved a crucial factor at breaking down the defence of the Samoans. But it wasn't a perfect display, nor could have he expected it to be with such limited preparation. One of his errors, a charged down kick, resulted in Samoa's left wing Alex Telea racing 40 metres for his side's try and in desperate attempts to clear the ball wide Mehrtens was also guilty in the second spell of a couple of rough passes.

But this was a night for him to stand tall – the injury picked up in Italy now confined to the past once and for all.

In the year's next two tests – against Scotland in Dunedin and Auckland – the All Blacks cruised to 62-31 and 36-12 wins. Cullen – with a four try haul at Carisbrook – again dominated the headlines. But Mehrtens' contribution didn't go unnoticed. Doug Golightly, writing in *The Truth* best summed up his contribution to the wins, which included points hauls of 22 and 11 respectively.

Said Golightly: "In the three tests this season Mehrtens has been in commanding form. Returning to Napier for the test against Manu Samoa after knee reconstruction, Mehrtens started tentatively but soon showed his class with a passing and kicking display that had authority stamped all over it. But the rustiness still showed as he tried to punt the ball too hard, rather than timing it, resulting in some kicks wobbling into touch or slicing off the side of his boot.

"There was no such rustiness at Carisbrook or Eden Park despite there being enough rain at the latter venue to ensure even the most proven water repellant was severely tested. Mehrtens dictated play at both venues despite suffering from slow service at the `Brook (and I don't blame Justin Marshall for that, but rather the tight five) to contribute to two emphatic All Black wins. But it was the second-half effort at Eden Park that saw Mehrtens at his best.

"Feeding off an intensely committed effort from the All Black pack, Mehrtens, alongside Marshall, punished the Scots who had a gale at their backs. That effort was a clear indicator to the Wallabies and Springboks that Mehrtens won't take a back seat to anyone. And with seven tests coming up against the current and former world champions it was one of the better signals All Black fans could have been given."

Mehrtens' form continued into the inaugural Tri-nations – a tournament involving the All Blacks, Australia and South Africa. The opening match for the New Zealanders was at Athletic Park against the Wallabies. In the wind, rain and mud the All Blacks put on a near faultless display as they won 43-6. And while the forward pack that day was sublime, Mehrtens had the spotlight firmly on him after the victory.

"Andrew Mehrtens was probably my man of the match," New Zealand's 1987 World Cup winning captain David Kirk said after the game. "His decision-making and accuracy in every thing he did were high class indeed. Certainly his forwards provided him with time and space, but he used that time to pass players into gaps, chip for his wings and direct play to the open spaces with precision."

ABOVE: Frank Bunce was one the stars of John Hart's first two years in charge.
PAGES 36 and 37: John Hart's stint as All Blacks boss couldn't have got off to a better start.
PAGE 39: Mehrtens could ignite a backline with one deft pass.

Despite missing the first three conversions Mehrtens scored 13 points, passing 200 points in just his 12th test – a New Zealand record. He now had 210 points, placing him second overall in points scored by an All Black after passing Allan Hewson (201 from 19 tests) and Don Clarke (207 from 31 tests) at Athletic Park. Predictably Mehrtens was quick to distance himself from the record post-game. Instead he looked to give credit to his teammates. But his performance was masterly. Into the southerly wind Mehrtens produced a number of delicate chip and grubber kicks so weighted that his own players had every chance of regaining possession. One led to halfback Justin Marshall's try after Jonah Lomu's 'slide-and-stand' piece of skill regathered the ball and sent Marshall clear. "It was pointless kicking the ball in the air too much," said Mehrtens. "You're not sure how accurate you'll be in a wind like that. You may as well keep it on the ground and make it slippery and difficult to play – apart from Jonah, of course, on the burst being able to pick up the ball like that. We've got very good skills and the boys showed them. The chasing was great as well – Jeff (Wilson) a couple of times lining up Matt Burke. It was a better option to keep the ball on the ground, and I learnt that from the Scottish test in Auckland where a couple of times I put it in the air behind Kenny Logan when it should have stayed on the ground."

Mehrtens also offered a tribute to his halfback partner Marshall. "Everyone says that seeing we're from Canterbury we should have a good partnership. We're good mates and everything like that, but we've still only

Mehrtens was quick to distance himself from the hype after breaking Grant Fox's record.

played 11 or 12 big games. I think every game we get better. It was probably to our advantage we had that game in Auckland in the conditions. That probably helped a lot. Then it comes back to the forwards doing their job – they gave Justin a hell of a platform. They cleaned out the Australians and gave him a lot of good ball."

Mehrtens would have done well to take the accolades because they were none coming his way after his next test – his first at Lancaster Park. The Springboks were beaten 15-11 – all of New Zealand's points coming from his boot – and while many in the team were targeted by the press afterwards Mehrtens bore the brunt of some negative copy from the greatest rugby writer of them all, veteran TP McLean.

"Andrew Mehrtens may well be lauded to the skies for placing all five of the New Zealand goals – and a nasty shiver of recollection of Carisbrook in 1959 went through my mind before the last kick which in effect settled the issue," McLean wrote in the *Sunday Star Times*. "But Mehrtens made an unacceptable number of errors in kicking into touch on the full, in kicking too deep from halfway or the 22m line and by these errors of judgment he much too often placed the All Blacks in the most serious of difficulties. Without doubt, the 'Boks were over-eager, sinning heavily in tackling from offside positions, and it was good luck that Mehrtens landed a sufficient number of goals for the match."

While Hart too was critical saying "he'll be quite happy to put behind him" Mehrtens would describe the game as bittersweet. Bitter because it was a flawed display and sweet because his first test at his home ground has seen the All Blacks beat the world champions. "I made six or seven bad mistakes that put us under pressure and they were right out in the open," he said. He was not happy particularly with 22 dropouts going out on the full, missing touch and having kicks charged down. But while a concern, they were areas he could work on and make more accurate. He admitted he was probably more nervous than usual because it was his first test on his home ground. He had gone to the toilet an inordinate number of times and had even felt like a return to the toilet as he ran on to the field. Not the ideal build up for test that was "the same sort of style of game (as the World Cup final). We had the same difficulty in getting absolutely hammered back at times. It was very physical and confrontational… yeah, the same sort of game. We were preparing ourselves for a war zone but until you're out there getting smashed you can't really picture it. That's what happened, we got hit hard."

Despite the criticism the reality was the All Blacks were now – thanks to two consecutive wins – only one victory away from securing the Tri-nations title. And with the next game due for Brisbane it was the ideal opportunity for the All Blacks to 'take care of business' before the grueling tour of South Africa which would include four tests against the old enemy – a sobering thought when remembering that the All Blacks' last try against the Springboks was Zinzan Brooke's at Athletic Park in 1994, three matches and 320 minutes ago.

But if they needed a pick-me-up before heading to the Republic, they got it at Suncorp Stadium with a last gasp 32-25 victory against the Wallabies. It was one of rugby's great escapes as the All Blacks had trailed by 13 points at one stage in the second half before a Mehrtens penalty sparked the comeback. And with the scores locked at 25-25 and the All Blacks on attack Mehrtens took the game by the scuff of the neck and inspired the unlikely win. Mehrtens ghosted through a gap after doubling around outside Frank Bunce, and then slipped a pass to Christian Cullen which had try written all over it. The fullback elected to ignore Jeff Wilson outside him and cut inside, only to be brought down short of the line. But Bunce had not stopped running, and he was crucially first there to snaffle Cullen's delicately placed ball and, with Josh Kronfeld providing the force, he pummeled his way over for the winning try.

"Obviously the pressure is on Harty to maintain a form team and Carlos has played very well. It doesn't help me reflecting that he got those opportunities because I was injured. But he is playing well and that's good for the team and it is a team game. I would never want anyone to do badly just for my own means."

"After the World Cup final I wasn't eager to risk everything on a dropped goal," Mehrtens said. "We practice moves at training all the time and hardly ever use them so I called one we'd worked at that very week. The Wallabies obviously didn't think we would go for a try. Frank Bunce put me into the gap and it was a wonderful sensation to realize I had two of the fastest players in the world – Christian Cullen and Jeff Wilson – in support. That try gave us all a huge buzz."

With the Tri-nations won, Hart praised the turnaround performance by Mehrtens from seven days earlier. Down 9-16 at halftime and then 9-22, the lackluster All Blacks sparked into action in the final 20 minutes with Mehrtens' accurate boot and his role in Bunce's sensational last minute try. "Call it an escape act but only great sides escape. These guys showed an incredible amount of heart out there. They were physically tired all week… the win over the Springboks had taken a lot out of them. The amount of mistakes reflected that. We turned over a lot of ball. I told them at halftime that they had to hang in there, win some ball and go forward. What a magnificent last 20 minutes. I was worried at 22-9 but I never count these guys out, they just have so much heart. You talk about leadership in these situations, well just look out there. I spoke to Andrew a lot during the week, but he responded very well. That was a great kicking performance out there."

By the time the All Blacks arrived in South Africa the psychological battle, so much a part of touring South Africa, has already started. Former Springbok Naas Botha was in the news after he predicted New Zealand would be whitewashed in the four tests in the Republic. The former first five-eighth had been in Australia and New Zealand with the Springboks for their two away Tri-nations tests and clearly wasn't impressed with the All Black win in Christchurch where the New Zealanders relied on Mehrtens' boot for their narrow victory.

The All Blacks began their tour with a midweek 32-21 win against a Boland Invitation XV at Worcester – a match that saw Taine Randell captain the All Blacks for the first time. But all the focus, naturally, was on the Newlands stadium in Cape Town for first of the four tests. Mehrtens summed up the mood in the All Blacks camp when, after being asked by a South African reporter if he was concerned the All Blacks hadn't scored a try against the 'Boks in three tests said: "I'd rather win against them without a try than lose scoring tries."

As it transpired the All Blacks – thanks to a stellar display from its pack – crossed for two touchdowns in the 29-18 win. Glen Osborne – playing for an injured Jonah Lomu – and prop Craig Dowd got the five pointers while Mehrtens added five penalties and two conversions.

If the All Blacks were looking to set the tone for up-coming tests, they succeeded. Former South African front rower Uli Schmidt said the main blow struck by the All Blacks was in the forwards. "South Africa prides its scrum but you've humiliated them now and I'm not so sure whether they can overcome that and come back in the series. I think you've kicked us where it hurts most; our front row was gone 15 minutes from the end. It was shattering… They destroyed us like they were feeding us poison gradually, then landed the final blow when your prop scored."

The win secured an unbeaten record in the Tri-nations but with three tests still to be played there was little celebration. The day after the midweek side beat Eastern Province 31-23, Mehrtens' tour was turned upside down when he was injured as the test side trained on the hard surface at Boet Erasmus Stadium in Port Elizabeth.

Mehrtens was flown to Johannesburg from Port Elizabeth for a minor operation soon after a medical scan revealed a slightly torn cartilage in his knee. The All Black management remained optimistic he would play again on tour, after having earlier feared a worse injury.

Mehrtens had fell in agony, clutching his right knee on which he had reconstruction surgery the previous year. He was carried to the sideline for ice treatment.

"It looked pretty grim," All Blacks doctor John Mayhew said at the time. "We were concerned he may have damaged the reconstruction of his anterior cruciate." Mayhew said the result of the scan was very reassuring as no damage had been done to areas reconstructed in 1995. "He has done some damage to the cartilage which these days is regarded as a relatively minor injury." A specialist operated on Mehrtens the following day to remove a two-centimetre piece of unwanted cartilage before he rejoined the team in Durban. His realistic target would be the final test in Johannesburg in just over two weeks' time.

"I wouldn't like to put an exact time to it but guys have been back on the field within 10 days of such surgeries," he told reporters. "The surgeon was quite surprised when he saw there was no swelling the next morning. And there was a good degree of movement in it. Just as well we got it done straight away. It was the best thing we could have done if I wanted to continue playing rugby, but further down the line I may risk arthritis. The ligament around the knee is intact."

Simon Culhane came into the test side allowing him to resume his old Southland combination with Justin Marshall. "He brings special qualities with him," Hart said of Culhane. "Simon is an unassuming, quietly spoken guy, but we're lucky to have him. He comes off a wonderful last test in Paris against the French last year and is an experienced player, a wonderful goal kicker and does a lot of the things Andrew Mehrtens does. We don't lose a lot with him coming in and he adds some special qualities to the team – he's a top player."

For his part Marshall, with a his tongue planted in his cheek said he might finally be listened to with Mehrtens out of the picture. "I might have to take more of a decision role and do a lot more myself. I'll have to take more responsibility with the calling and try and dominate more.

"Simon – he's a good player, great to fit in with and it's just a matter of communicating. I usually can't get a word in with Mehrts out there but I have to be a talker. I can see things the forwards can't because they've got their heads in rucks and sometimes I can read things that the first fives can't see so I have to keep chatting away."

Culhane proved his worth helping guide the All Blacks to a 23-19 win. Culhane landed two penalties and kicked a conversion in a test that saw Jeff Wilson, Christian Cullen and Zinzan Brooke all score vital tries. Culhane equaled Mehrtens' record by scoring his test 100 points in five matches. But it was his general play and tackling that impressed Hart. Culhane's pressure-relieving kicks to the corners were vital. "The more I looked at the video of the game the more impressed I've got," Hart said. "His defence work was superb. For anyone to come into the test side and do what he did was quite outstanding. Sure, he might have missed a couple of close kicks. I don't think he missed touch once. He had some tremendous tackles, he took Ruben Kruger out of the game several times."

After the midweekers has disposed of Western Transvaal 31-0, attention turned to Pretoria and the chance for the All Blacks to do what they had never done before – win a test series in South Africa. Teams in 1928, 1949, 1960, 1970 and 1976 had tried and failed. And amazingly Mehrtens – just a week after his injury – was training again and available for selection for the test at Loftus Versfeld Stadium. Hart delayed the naming of the team to give Mehrtens every chance to make the side. "My personal view is that we don't need to take a risk," Hart said. "We've got to be very confident that Andrew Mehrtens is 110 per cent. This is an awfully big test match."

Ultimately Mehrtens lost his battle for selection. "We are lucky we've got plenty for resource backup," said Hart. "You'd be very happy with Simon Culhane in Durban. We know what we'll get out of Simon. Andrew Mehrtens is a match-winner; he's a class act. They're different players and if Andrew was right, then obviously he'd play. But there is a lot of judgment on what is right. It's not the knee being right. It's the fact that coming back from the operation he missed a bit of training, missed a bit of time with us – the mental preparation is not quite as good as maybe others who have been thinking a lot more about playing. Realistically, I don't think he saw himself playing this week."

The depth of New Zealand's talent pool couldn't have been summed up any better than at Loftus. The test – and the series – was famously won 33-26 with Zinzan Brooke getting a try along with a brace from Jeff Wilson. And while Culhane had converted all three tries and landed a penalty, he was pulled from the action with a wrist injury in the 63rd minute. On came Wellington's Jon Preston – equally at home at halfback or first five – to land two more penalties before Brooke's cheeky dropped goal completed the scoring. "It's been nerve-wracking watching the All Blacks play," Mehrtens said. "It sends big shivers down the spine when they are out on the paddock. You just sit there and hope for so much the whole time and you end up more mentally drained than when you actually play."

Mehrtens wouldn't have to watch for much longer with Hart calling him up for the fourth and final test at Johannesburg's Ellis Park. Some in the media thought that Mehrtens should have played for the mid-weekers against Griqualand West (a game drawn 18-18) but Hart never entertained the idea despite two weeks of inactivity. "Andrew Mehrtens has nothing to prove by playing in the midweek game," said Hart emphatically. "We know his abilities and that he can step into the test arena. I would rather keep him fresh for the test than risk him against Griqualand. It is more a question of how he gets through the week at practice."

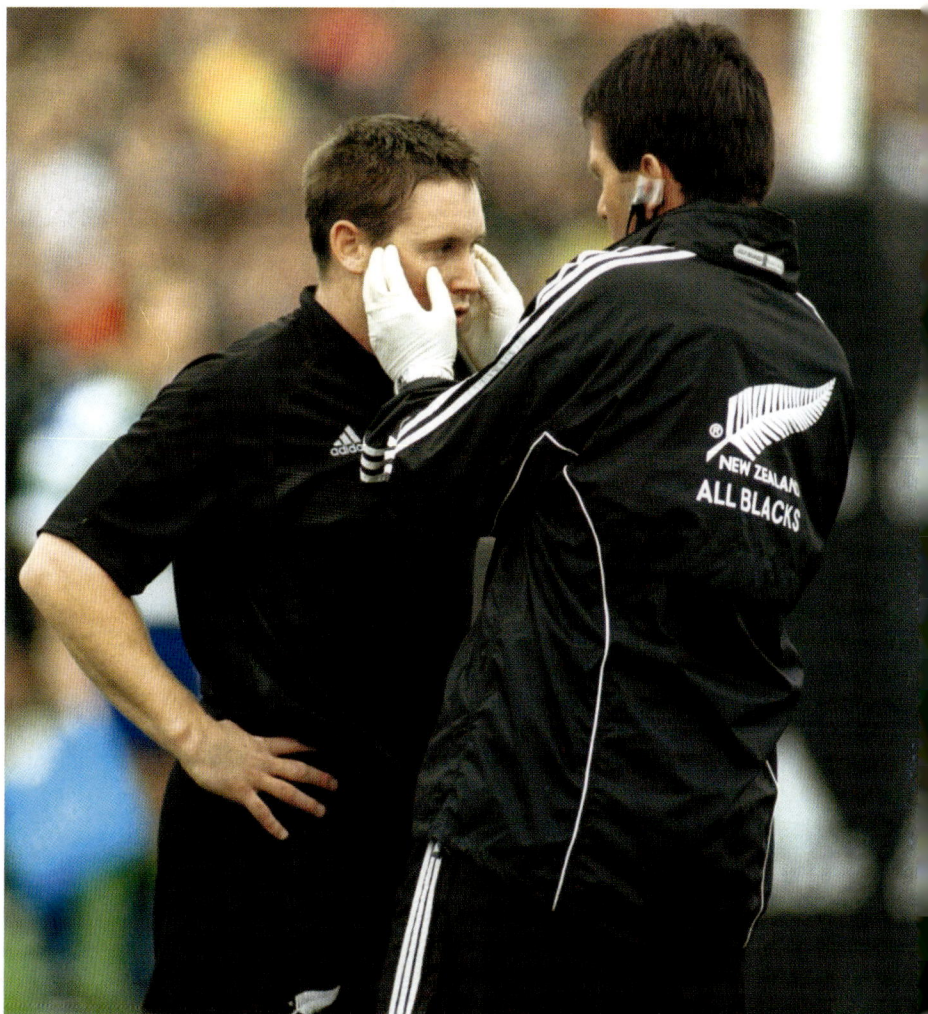

ABOVE: Some said Mehrtens was fragile – here he is attended to by Dr John Mayhew.
FOLLOWING PAGES: Walter 'Waltza' Little was the perfect foil for Mehrtens in the All Blacks backline.

Before the test Naas Botha – who predicted the 'Boks would beat the All Blacks 4-0 – said he rated Mehrtens as the best first five-eighths in world rugby. "His punts are potent, keeping opponents stretched and his goal kicking is top notch. He varies his play shrewdly and his defence is more than adequate." Asked to come up with All Black candidates for a World XV, Botha nominated seven, headed by Mehrtens. The others were backs Jonah Lomu, despite his poor tour of South Africa, and centre Frank Bunce, loose forwards Michael Jones and Zinzan Brooke – "the best No 8 in the world" – captain Sean Fitzpatrick and lock Ian Jones.

The battered and tired All Blacks couldn't lift for the last test of a long year. The Springboks won 32-22 and while the All Blacks scored three tries through Sean Fitzpatrick, Walter Little and Justin Marshall it could be argued the difference was Mehrtens missing five shots at goal – two from in front of the posts - even though he belted one tremendous kick over from 60m.

All that was forgotten quickly though as the All Blacks returned home from their triumphant series win. Hart had done what he was charged with when he took on the job – he took the team built by Laurie Mains and put right the wrong that was the 1995 World Cup final.

RIVALRIES. It doesn't matter which sport you talk about it's the rivalries that excite us the most. Ali v Foreman. Bjorn v Mac. Spurs v Arsenal. Tiger v Phil. Bulldogs v Eels. Irene v Liz. And, of course, rugby has always been rich in rivalries. Tremain v Kirkpatrick. Deans v Hewson. Mehrtens v Spencer…

FROM the time he made age group representative sides in Horowhenua it was clear Carlos Spencer was a rugby phenomenon. At 16, while still at Waiopehu College in Levin, he entered first class representative rugby in the 1992 NPC third division. A year later, aged only 17, he

gave further glimpses of his rare promise when in an early season Ranfurly Shield challenge he scored a spectacular solo try in Horowhenua-Kapiti's defeat by Auckland.

Graham Henry was coaching Auckland at the time and was clearly taken by the youngster's ability. It was hardly a coincidence that the following year Spencer moved to Auckland. While it took the youngster some time to adjust to the big city pace of Auckland, he soon became a regular feature of Auckland representative sides in succession to Grant Fox. In 1994 he also came into competition with Mehrtens for the first time when both were included in the New Zealand Colts squad, with Spencer being preferred for the main games.

The duo were linked again in 1995 when, after Mehrtens was injured on the tour to France and Italy, Spencer replaced him. And in 1996 the pair toured South Africa with Spencer playing the midweek games against Eastern Province and Western Transvaal.

But by the time the international season of 1997 rolled around Mehrtens' hold on the black jersey looked tenuous. Mehrtens had ended the 1996 domestic season playing solid rugby for a Canterbury team that lost its NPC semi-final to Counties. Spencer on the other hand had played brilliantly and laid down his test credentials leading Auckland to the title – months after he'd done the same in the Super 12 with the Blues. Intriguingly both players were included in the New Zealand Barbarians' tour to the UK at the end of the year. "I think New Zealand is fortunate to have two such fine young players," Henry said. "Carlos is probably the better field player, but Andrew's the better kicker. Carlos now has to work on his kicking and has to start kicking goals."

John Hart certainly didn't foresee the presence of both Spencer and Mehrtens causing a dilemma. Hart did not see the merits of Spencer versus Mehrtens becoming an issue in New Zealand similar to that when Grant Fox and Frano Botica were competing against each other in the late 1980s. "I think it's good we've got two such outstanding young players available to us at first five-eighths. Both have considerable skills but in different areas."

Hart made it clear the short tour had been agreed to to allow him to prepare for the 1997 test season. And he sent an early message when Spencer was selected for the opening game against England's Northern Counties at Huddersfield alongside All Blacks Christian Cullen, Glen Osborne, Alama Ieremia, Jonah Lomu, Lee Stensness, Carlos Spencer, Justin Marshall, Taine Randell, Andrew Blowers, Glenn Taylor, Robin Brooke, Dylan Mika, Mark Allen, Sean Fitzpatrick and Olo Brown. The game would be very one-sided, the New Zealanders winning 86-0 with Spencer kicking seven conversions and scoring a try before Mehrtens was brought on for the last portion of the game.

For the game against England, Mehrtens was selected ahead of Spencer and he moved quickly to dispel any angst between the two. "It's a good situation to be in," he told the *Evening Post*. "It's good for all of us. There's no animosity in the squad at all, and certainly there's no chance of anyone in the team taking their position for granted. There is depth there now, which is good for the team. With the tactical substitution rules I can't expect to play 80 minutes, or even 20 minutes. I would expect Carlos to play at some stage. That's the other good thing about this squad. We can slot anyone in and do the same things."

Mehrtens got the start but it would be Spencer who produced a moment of brilliance to give the Barbarians a 34-19 at Twickenham. The win was built on a superb performance by the tight five and punishing defence, but it was Spencer's individual skill that turned the game after he came on as a replacement for Mehrtens with 22 minutes left in the game. He arrived on the pitch with the Barbarians trailing 16-19 and one of his first acts was to kick a penalty to level at 19-19 before he added another after a period of sustained pressure to put them in front. With five minutes left, Spencer ripped the England defence apart with a searing solo run. Running to his right from a ruck, Spencer feigned to pass outside but then spotted a narrow gap, and darted into it, broke through two defenders then accelerated clear and sprinted 30 metres to score. He converted the try, and the Barbarians were clear at 29-19.

Such was the response to Spencer's performance, some in the media had him rated as the best first five – Mehrtens' tactical performance at Twickenham seemingly forgotten. Hart, was quick to go into bat for the incumbent. "I think he is a class act," said Hart of Mehrtens. "In the context, Andrew Mehrtens' display at Twickenham was quite outstanding. You've got to realise he played the game at a time when we were under pressure. England had a full head of steam and he created many opportunities for the team. And while Carlos' was a great individual try, don't forget Andrew Blowers' try which was totally made by Mehrtens." Hart conceded that Spencer's efforts had been notable. He singled out the Aucklander's renewed confidence and huge talent as the main positives. "But he's still got some work to do. He had three kicks charged down in the space of 20-odd minutes and people tend to forget those sorts of things."

While the pressure was on Mehrtens in 1997 – you wouldn't have known it. After missing the first three games of the Super 12 he finally made his debut in the round four game against the Chiefs. His 11 points helped them to a 24-15 win. The new Crusaders coach, Wayne Smith, was rapped. "What can you say. That's why he is such a wonderful player, coming back from such a bad injury to produce a performance like that."

For his part Mehrtens was less than happy with his first 40 minutes, which he put down to finding his

ABOVE: John Hart was all smiles in 1997 – it wouldn't last...
PAGE 50: Sean Fitzpatrick's days as All Blacks skipper were numbered.

feet back at this level, but was pleased to have finished strongly, and ecstatic that the team had come up with such a vital win. "I got through the game, so I'm happy. I was more nervous about the result really, than I was about my leg," he told the *Sunday Star Times*. Asked whether he thought Hart would be relieved at his performance, Mehrtens responded: "He probably thought I looked like a sloth. The forwards were all going a lot quicker than me. But I'm pleased just to have got through it. Some things will come with time and as I get more confidence on the leg that will help."

Two days later, on April Fools Day, Mehrtens was at his mischievous best with prank which landed him in hot water with his mum. People listening to radio station *NewsTalk ZB* were shocked to hear Canterbury rugby coach Wayne Smith confirm a 'rumour' that Mehrtens had signed a $1m deal to play Super 12 rugby for Natal. The rumour was given added credibility when breakfast show host John Dunne apparently rang a South African reporter who said the deal was all over the news. To really irk listeners the reporter said as Mehrtens was born in Durban he would be eligible to play for the Springboks. Immediately the radio station's lines were jammed with callers wanting to wish Mehrtens well and talk about a replacement.

The big problem was that Sandra Mehrtens, Andrew's mother, was one of the many people who swallowed the joke hook, line, and sinker. Mrs Mehrtens was absolutely stunned when she heard the radio report and got very steamed up. "I can laugh now but at the time I felt like crying," she said. "Oooh, he's a little rogue!" When her son rang to confess it was a joke, he could not believe his mother had fallen for it. Mehrtens was surprised about how many people were taken in by the joke, which was hatched by the radio station. "I was put up to it," Mehrtens said. "The more people who bought into it, the worse I felt. Most people who know me would know I don't want to leave Canterbury." Mehrtens said he would steer clear of his parents for a week "or until I need a good feed" to give

his mother time to recover. For her part, Sandra said her son could expect a good clip around the ear next time he visits. "What a cheeky little beggar he is," she said.

It is worth noting that to tell the story of Andrew Mehrtens it needs to be stressed that while he could easily win people over with his quick wit and sense of humor, he was equally at home talking about the serious issues facing the game. He was, and still is, one of the game's great students. Despite only having two years experience in the black jersey, he was, in 1997, the first professional player to talk about the pressure that would come on players with the increasing schedule put forward for the All Blacks. It would be a fight taken up by the likes of Justin Marshall and Tana Umaga in the future but Mehrtens was before his time. And days after the April's Fools Day prank he had the rugby public thinking after an interview in *The Press*.

He joined John Hart in criticising the growing number of rugby tests being loaded on to the All Blacks saying it was detrimental to the players and the public to saturate the season with showcase rugby. Hart earlier pleaded for the All Blacks not to play any more than five end-of-season games in Britain. That program included three tests. Now the All Blacks were set to play eight games, including four tests on consecutive weekends. Hart, concerned about injuries, burnout and the difficulties players face in maintaining their peak in such demanding programs, met NZRU to try to encourage the union to map out easier international programs.

Mehrtens refused to be silent on the issue. "It's not quite right at the moment. We are committed to five home tests a year, plus one in South Africa and one in Australia. Then there's an end-of-year tour as well. The Welsh test was added on last year and just recently the Irish too. That's a hell of a lot of rugby. There's a rugby operations committee in the New Zealand Rugby Football Union and a players' committee have had input to that. We met last year but that's the last I have heard of it. They (the NZRU) are not expected to consult everyone, but I don't know who they did consult.

England has a lot of money and obviously the NZRU, as a business, has got to look at their books too. It's hard finding the balance but it's not heavily in favour of the All Blacks at the moment. They will realise soon they are not getting the best out of the players by playing more games."

Mehrtens, in a unprecedented attack on the NZRU in the pro era, argued that there was a need for more consultation with the players required to play the increasing number of tests on top of club rugby, NPC and the Super 12. Leading All Blacks, he said, were concerned two years ago that too many NZRU decisions affecting them were being made without their knowledge. Mehrtens said the players needed more feedback. "It's a difficult time for the NZRU, which has a lot to do, and maybe it's going to be this way for the first few years until everything gets sorted out – until we get used to the post-amateur era. It seems the NZRU gets pushed around (by other nations). The English teams that come out here get a large say in what their itinerary is and all of a sudden we get shoved around and told there is an Irish test over there. I think the Home Unions are wielding too much power. You wonder how much thought goes into the decisions to quickly throw in more test matches. We just hear about it afterwards and there are not many avenues for us to express what we think. But it seems not a lot is being listened to. A lot of All Blacks might feel if they complain about too many games they would feel guilty because they are now being well paid and should do what they are told."

Mehrtens was on a roll. Next his target was referees saying if players lose form in the Super 12 they are dropped and he believed referees in the competition should be similarly judged. Mehrtens said he felt the general standard of refereeing in the Super 12 left much to be desired and wondered whether the powers of the touch judges could be extended further. "I think the video should be used to analyse referees' performances and if they regularly make more than say

five obvious mistakes then they should be downgraded as their penalty. Touch judges seem to have so much input now that they could be wired up to be in contact with the referees and keep an eye on three or four things each side of rucks when referees are watching those. The touch judges have some powers now so let's standardise it and have them talking to the referee all the time. If the referee and touch judges are wired then that's six eyes watching what's happening. If the referee has plugs in his ears then he won't have to listen to the likes of me or Fitzy (Sean Fitzpatrick) talking to him."

All of that was going on days before the Crusaders headed north for a match up with the Blues – and the personal duel between Mehrtens and Spencer was being written about on the back of every newspaper in the country. The Blues assistant coach, the firey Mac McCallion, ensured plenty of pre-game talk was focused on the first fives when he said the Blues would target Mehrtens. "We don't think he is as fit as he can be, he still looks a bit shaky and maybe he isn't quite right yet," McCallion said. "We will have our guys go in and have a good look to see if he is all right and see if we can put him off his game. Our loosies will be keeping an eye on him."

The Blues won a tight encounter 29-28 but the consensus amongst the country's scribes was that Mehrtens won the one-on-one encounter with Spencer. Certainly his coach thought he did. Said Smith: "There's been a debate raging, particularly in Auckland, and I think he answered the question. I thought Mehrtens and Justin Marshall were superb. If you are the best, it is a bit like a gunslinger I suppose, there are always questions about you. But he takes the pressure really well."

Patrick McKendry, writing in the Sunday News was gushing in his praise of the Cantabrian. "Andrew Mehrtens scored a knockout over challenger Carlos Spencer in the battle for the All Black No 10 jersey. His kicking, both at goal and for touch, was accurate, and he constantly pressured the Blues' defence with his running and passing. Mehrtens clearly outplayed

Spencer." Mehrtens didn't buy into the hype however. "I don't tend to read too much into anything that's said about Carlos and me," he said. "It's hard to have a match-up one on one as first fives because it all depends on the ball you get. It gets quite annoying because it's sometimes made out that it's a personal thing as well. I get on fine with Carlos; we just go out and try to do our own thing as well as we can. I was happy with some things and there are some things to improve on. Carlos has been scoring so many tries lately it was nice to not see him score for a change."

The Crusaders would finish in the top half of the Super 12 for the first time at the conclusion of the season – a season where the Blues would win the competition for the second consecutive year. Hart had earlier shown his desire for change in this new year. Seven players who were a part of the historic South African jaunt were left out of the All Blacks' first training camp of 1997. Phil Coffin and Con Barrell, loose forward Todd Blackadder, midfield back Tabai Matson, centre Scott McLeod, wing Eric Rush and fullback Matthew Cooper were all missing from the Taupo camp in February.

So some where surprised when he named Mehrtens in the shadow test side for the NZ Barbarians games against New Zealand 'A'. Spencer would wear the No 10 for the As.

The game would be an uneventful one with both first fives playing well but not spectacularly so the status quo – Mehrtens in the starting XV – would be restored for the opening test of the season against Fiji at North Harbour.

Mehrtens in a classical pose kicking at Twickenham.

It would be a game remembered for two celebratory stories and one tragic one. As Taine Randell and Tana Umaga made their debuts in the 71-5 thrashing of the Fijians the outstanding flanker Michael Jones was cut down after tearing a tendon in his knee. It would keep him out of test rugby for a year. Another injured 20 minutes from the finish was Mehrtens who tore a hamstring. "It just popped," Mehrtens said. "I've actually been working more on my left hamstring which has been a bit tight this week. I've had tired legs at times in the last couple of weeks, but it's a combination of everything, I've got to work more on my flexibility I think. I was trying to chase Taine Randell down the blindside but he just took off too quick for me."

The injury meant Mehrtens was unavailable for the first of the two tests against Argentina. Spencer would get his first test start for the All Blacks and that had Gonzalo Quesada, Argentina's playmaker, worried. He said he would have preferred facing Mehrtens as Spencer's unpredictability, made him a difficult player to hold down. "You don't know what he's doing, when he's doing what – too unpredictable," he said. "Andrew is a very steady player. You can read him. You know what he will do, although it may be hard trying to stop him doing it. At least you can see it coming from Andrew. Spencer just comes. He's here and then he's there, and next thing he's gone – good-bye."

In an effort to keep the pressure off Spencer, Hart originally leaned towards Christian Cullen taking the shots at Athletic Park but as the test got closer he said the choice was Spencer's. "If he wants to take out

An injury to Mehrtens opened the door for his great rival Carlos Spencer.

Andrew Mehrtens as the All Black test first five-eighths then he has to be a goal kicker. If Carlos tells me he wants to be the goal kicker, then he will be the goal kicker," Hart said. "It is his call really. I don't want to put pressure on Carlos in his first test but I've watched him all week and I believe he's in great shape and will handle anything thrown at him. Carlos has had a lot more kicking practice this year than Christian."

Spencer took up Hart's challenge and laid one down firmly at Mehrtens' feet, as *Sunday News*'s 'Carlossus' headline suggested. His 33 points in the All Blacks 93-8 victory was an All Blacks record for points in a test in New Zealand. The previous best was 28 by Mehrtens against Canada at Eden Park in 1995. That was also Mehrtens' test debut. It was also the second highest points total by an All Black in a test. Simon Culhane scored 45 against Japan at the 1995 World Cup.

Spencer's performance was good enough to convince Hart to stick with him for the second test against the Argies in Hamilton. Mehrtens, who was fit again, had to be content with a place on the bench where he took Jon Preston's place. "It is not a selection decision," Hart spun after announcing the team. "The medical team believe if they can spend a full week with Andrew then they can have him near 100 percent by Saturday. We want to him to continue his rehabilitation and be ready for consideration for the test against Australia."

As it was Mehrtens was pulled from the bench before the test and Spencer continued his fine form setting up a battle royal for the pair to battle out the first five selection war for the Tri-nations. Spencer, despite missing three kicks at goal, provided 20 of the All Blacks' points in the 62-10 win. It was clear though, at this stage of the season, Hart still favoured Mehrtens. He selected him for the opening Bledisloe Cup game against Australia at Lancaster Park. But three days before the test Mehrtens limped from a training session clutching his troublesome hamstring.

It meant the local fans were robbed of seeing their two favourite All Black sons of the day – Marshall and Mehrtens take the field. The two were like chalk and cheese – Marshall a street fighter to Mehrtens' choir boy reputation – but they played their roles brilliantly as the *Christchurch Press*' John Brooks discovered in the build up to the test. The duo, he wrote, are deadly serious when they fill their pivotal roles behind the All Black forwards. Most other times it is their ability to quip and counter-quip which generates the relaxation of mind so essential for sportsmen performing at the highest level of competition.

Wrote Brooks: Encountering them for the first time is just like wandering on to the set of a '*Seinfeld*' rehearsal. Marshall was trying on a pair of new golf shoes in Geoff Clarke's pro shop at the Russley Club. "I think I'll try a size smaller," he said to Clarke. "My feet seem to be shrinking."

"Unlike your head," muttered Mehrtens, right on cue.

A poster in the Wilding Park pavilion once welcomed punters to a sports forum featuring Mehrtens at the Edgeware Tennis Club, of which he was a member. "Come and have your say," said the poster. "If you can get a word in." The All Black first five had now met someone who not only gets a word in, but also complements him by uttering every alternate line. Justin Marshall, from Mataura shattered the myth that most Southlanders are dour. He had the same laconic humour as Mehrtens, and meeting the pair is like being hit alternatively by Holyfield and Tyson, except that the experience is much sweeter.

"Banter is part of the team culture," explained Mehrtens. "But we laugh at ourselves, too. If you can't do that then everyone will laugh at you."

"Humour helps teamwork, and that means everyone's on the same level," said Marshall. "But we certainly don't enjoy missing out on any jokes. However, you have to be mindful of those players who wouldn't appreciate having a prank pulled on them in the build-up to a big game. They would probably think we were two little shits."

Interestingly, Marshall admitted to becoming nervous and withdrawn two days out from a test, whereas Mehrtens exuded good humour. "If I get too noisy he (Marshall) takes to me," said Mehrtens.

"Like the time I threw a ball at him, and he pulled a hamstring trying to stop it," joked Marshall.

Mehrtens can field that jibe in the spirit of good humour. The two young All Blacks realise that the higher the level of rugby they are playing, the more modification is needed of the funny business. When the Bledisloe Cup is at stake the jokes will be left in the changing room until later. Then the cork can pop, just as it did in one important game which Marshall missed because of a long-running groin injury. Mehrtens was asked for a comment on television, and, looking directly down the camera's barrel, dedicated the victory to Marshall.

"We just hope, Justin, that you didn't strain your other leg hobbling from the couch to the fridge."

The two players had good communication on the field and the communication was evident in most activities they undertook, such as their public relations efforts, especially with the kids and the sick. "Those things are part and parcel of our life now," said Marshall. "If it ever starts to drag I just think of how much better it is than working a nine-to-five job."

Mehrtens: "Some say we're just a couple of smart-arses, but we're not. We are just enjoying life." He paused. "I suppose we can be smart-arses at times, too."

ABOVE: Mehrtens was always looking to get one over the media – although this time it was more luck than plan!
RIGHT: Mehrtens never shyed away from the spotlight – he thrived under it.

Then it was time for the big question: Who is the person they would most like to meet? Mehrtens: "I thought of someone the other day, but now I've forgotten who it was." Marshall: "That's a tough one."

Mehrtens, prompting: "What about Pol Pot?" (the former brutal leader of the Khmer Rouge in Cambodia).

Marshall: "Yeah, that will do – Pol Pot."

Then he looks at Mehrtens a trifle dubiously. "I won't get into trouble for saying that, will I?"

That Mehrtens could be so relaxed despite his injury woes and the pressure coming from Spencer says much for the man and his ability to switch in and out of the intensity required to be an great All Black. The weekend would be a mixed one from Mehrtens' point of view. Spencer would go a long way to melting the Lancaster Park crowd with a stellar performance in the 30-13 win against the Wallabies. Hart was certainly impressed saying: "I thought in terms of tactics he had a good all-round game. Andrew Mehrtens is a big loss, but I don't think any longer Carlos Spencer sits on Mehrtens' shoulder. They're both such good players and it's good to have them both." The following day at Rugby Park, Mehrtens had to prove his fitness for the trip to South Africa by getting though a club game for Old Boys against Sydenham. He did enough to make the trip to Johannesburg. "It was pretty low key really and we didn't want him to overdo it," Hart said. "He did what we wanted and that was to show us he had confidence to get out and play."

Once in the Republic for the beginning of the Tri-

Mehrtens finds something funny while Pita Alatini and Mark Robinson are all concentration.

nations Mehrtens impressed with an encouraging effort in a six-kilometre time trial at a game park and looked a good bet to get the start at Ellis Park. But in a massive disappointment to Mehrtens, Hart opted for Spencer. "In the end it came down to the fact that Carlos has played a lot more rugby in recent times than Andrew," Hart said. "Andrew is coming back from five weeks without a game of any intensity. We think Carlos is conditioned at the moment to play test rugby."

Mehrtens couldn't, and didn't complain. Spencer had earned his place in the team but Mehrtens knew that this was the first time Spencer had been picked ahead of him on form and form alone. As debate between the south and north fans raged in New Zealand, Mehrtens pledged to support his teammate. And Spencer, full of confidence, responded to the vote of confidence with a try, three penalties and three conversions in a titanic 35-32 victory.

That performance meant there was little chance of Mehrtens getting the start in the next test, against Australia, in front of 90,119 screaming fans at the famed Melbourne Cricket Ground. Spencer was looking more comfortable with each outing. What's more, he was producing some superlative goal kicking, the one area that was of a real concern to the All Blacks through the absence of Mehrtens. At the MCG he coolly slotted seven goals from seven attempts, including a 48m effort to get the All Blacks on the board in the opening minutes of the one-sided 33-18 win. "You've got to take your hat off to Carlos Spencer," Hart said after the test. "He's not been a goal kicker until this year, but he at last accepted the message he's got to be a kicker. Carlos is now probably the equal as a goal kicker (to Mehrtens) so it comes down to playing form."

Mehrtens said it was hard hearing those words. "Obviously the pressure is on 'Harty' to maintain a form team and Carlos has played very well. It doesn't help me reflecting that he got those opportunities because I was injured. But he is playing well and that's good for the team and it is a team game. I would never want anyone to do badly just for my own means."

As the All Blacks faced a bye-week in the Tri-nations before the next game against the 'Boks at Eden Park, Mehrtens donned the Bay of Plenty colours for a night. He played against Auckland to get some valuable game time but there was never a chance that he would displace Spencer in that player's first test at his home ground – a test where he would score 25 points in the All Blacks' 55-35 win. Mehrtens was given the last 13 minutes of the test and headed to Dunedin for the last game of the Tri-nations against Australia as very much the All Blacks' No 2 first five.

Spencer, who had fought off a hamstring strain leading up to the Carisbrook test, put up only an average performance in the game, won 36-24. And it didn't take long for Mehrtens' supporters to come to the fore. The late Hedley Mortlock, writing for *Sunday News*, summed up for many when he suggested Mehrtens could, or should, be brought back into the frame sooner rather than later. "There is some irony here because Spencer was outplayed by his opposite David Knox except for place kicking," he wrote. "The All Blacks backs yesterday desperately needed the quick hands and the inventiveness of a Knox or, dare I say it, an Andrew Mehrtens. Last week the All Blacks looked like monsters from another planet. Now I'm not so sure. The path to the next World Cup might be a lot more rocky than we think." And Phil Gifford, writing in the *Sunday Star Times* added his weight to the Mehrtens/Spencer debate: "On Friday night, a great coach told me that there is a basic flaw in the All Black backline with Carlos Spencer taking the ball flat-footed and sometimes taking several paces before he passes. 'Last year Andrew Mehrtens took the ball on the run and so he generated speed from there. He passed in one stride and that gave a player like Cullen the time he needed when he hit the line. Now Alama Ieremia and Frank Bunce are cramped when they get the ball and the movements break down.'"

Mehrtens did plenty to encourage his fan base in the NPC where Canterbury's march to the title was sublime. It included a 21-15 semifinal win against the mighty Aucklanders – a result that ended Auckland's four-year NPC reign. Alas, an injured Spencer was missing from the game, but no one could doubt Mehrtens was fighting hard to win back his starting slot in the All Blacks on the end of year tour. He had to fight hard after a horror night at North Harbour earlier in the season when he slotted only two of his nine goal kicking attempts home. By the end of the semifinal he'd kicked 14 of his last 15 place kicks. "I'm feeling more comfortable about my goal kicking," Mehrtens told *The Press*' Bob Schumacher. "Rather than worry about the mechanics or about technique I'm just kicking the ball and it is coming off the boot nicely. Inevitably, the more you think about something the more it ends up not going well. I'm relaxing and just kicking it – that's the best advice I've had from anyone."

Mehrtens did listen and accept advice, however, from Canterbury coach Robbie Deans, himself a champion goal kicker, who is the province's most prolific points-scorer with 1641. Deans emphasised the importance of doing the groundwork. "He said the more base work you do on kicking, the more it enables you to relax in a game knowing that you have that base behind you. That gives you confidence generally for you can't play a good all-round game if you're worried about one aspect of it."

Mehrtens took a further step towards winning back his All Blacks jersey in the NPC final against Counties-Manukau as the Cantabs won their first title in 14 years with an emphatic 44-13 win. On the historic night Mehrtens kicked four conversions to advance his season's total to 28, four more than the previous NPC Canterbury mark of 24 set by present coach, Deans. Mehrtens, with his second conversion, had moved past Greg Coffey and into fourth place on the all-time Canterbury points-scoring table with 684 points. But Mehrtens, while thrilled with Canterbury's

achievement, admitted his thoughts were immediately focused on the tour to Ireland, England and Wales.

"Even celebrating the win on Sunday and Monday, I always had this (tour) in the back of my mind," he said. "So I didn't go too hard. The title is something I'll look back on more next year and take more satisfaction in it because my focus has gone straight on the tour. While Canterbury played really well, I wasn't going overboard in my own form. There is a lot more I can be doing. I don't think I'm playing as well as I can. It's a matter of getting my speed up as well as my work rate. I guess I've strung 12 games together without an injury which is the first time in two or three years. So I'm pretty rapt about that. Now (the All Blacks) want to go over there, and the ideal would be to go unbeaten. Personally, I want to work as hard as I can on my own stuff. If that's good enough to be in the test team, then wonderful."

Hart gave him first shot at the test jersey on the tour to England, Ireland and Wales when he picked him in the tour's first game against Llanelli. "Andrew Mehrtens is getting this game and Carlos Spencer will get the next game, so you can't read too much into this selection," Hart told reporters. "Everyone will get an opportunity before the first test, every position is up for grabs. But the majority of our test team should come from this first game."

With the country very much focused on the battle for the No 10 jersey Mehrtens addressed the press again – trying to convince them the team came first. "Carlos is playing very well at the moment, but I try not to consider our rivalry as a personal thing," he said. "I won't be playing the game starting to think about myself as such, I just want to put in a good performance for the team as a whole."

The Llanelli game gained more significance the day before the contest when skipper Sean Fitzpatrick pulled out of the game with a knee injury. He'd aggravated the injury during the Tri-nations and hadn't been the same player since. Pulling out of this game was the first real clue that his time leading the All Blacks was coming to an end. And with Zinzan Brooke also on the way out the All Blacks were very much at the crossroads.

Justin Marshall would be given the captaincy for the Llanelli game which was won 81-3. Christian Cullen stole the show with a four try haul while Mehrtens – who looked sharp behind a dominating pack – struggled with his goal kicking converting only four shots from his ten attempts. But the low conversion rate was put down to the unfamiliar Reebok ball that was used on the night and Mehrtens was named in the test side to play against Ireland. Carlos Spencer, along with Josh Kronfeld – the two players dropped from the last test four months earlier against Australia – were not . Said Hart: "Andrew Mehrtens offers the dimension we are looking for. Hopefully his goal-kicking will be rectified." The other change was at hooker where Fitzpatrick's knee meant a rare start for Norm Hewitt.

Mehrtens was rapped with his recall and glad not to be on the bench again. "It stretches your nerves. I take my hat off to people who come off the bench. I did find it difficult coming out of South Africa and going to Melbourne and not being used to the support role. I worked hard on my game and I guess for this week it has been good enough."

Hart's decision paid off as Mehrtens celebrated his return to the test lineup with a record-breaking display in the 63-15 win over Ireland at Lansdowne Road. Mehrtens only needed one opportunity to re-establish himself as the country's best first five and he took it in

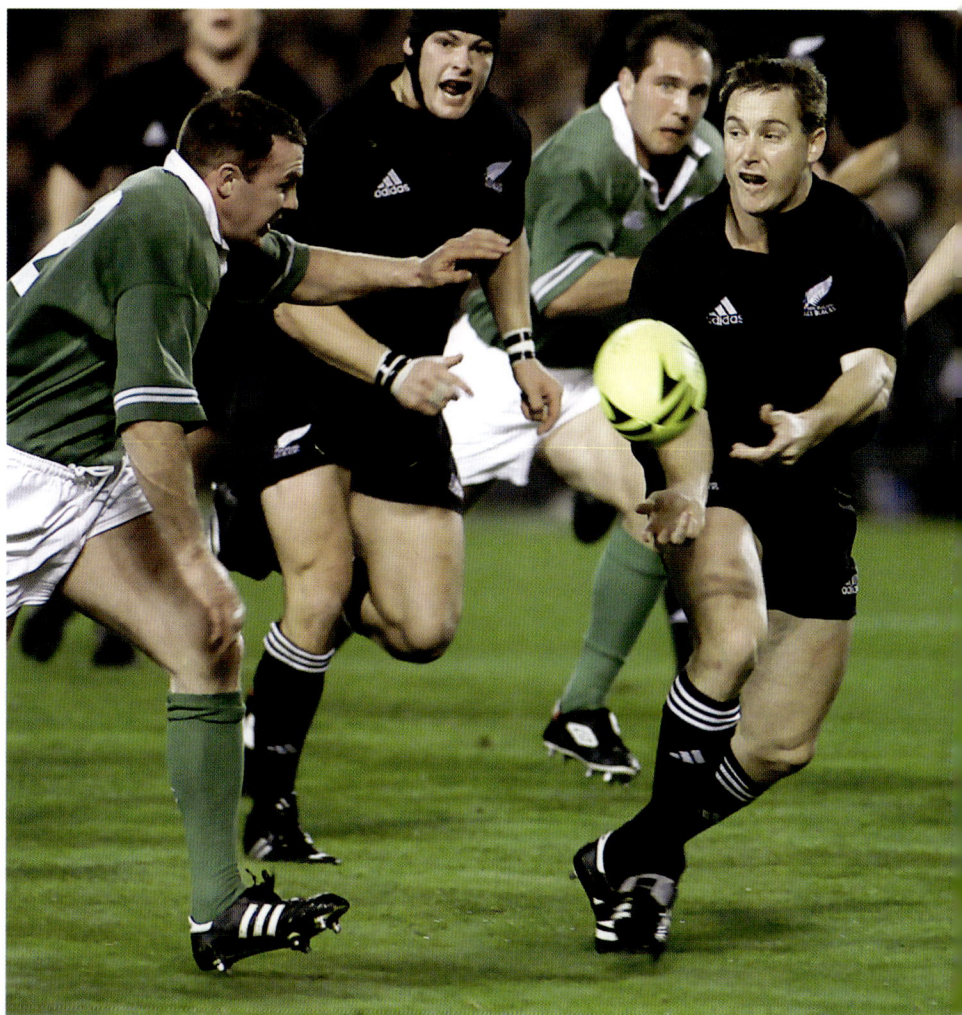

ABOVE: Mehrtens – pictured here towards the end of his international career – impressed Hart with his versatility.
FOLLOWING PAGE: Mehrtens in a classic pose – the man who enjoyed life (and rugby).

style. It helped his cause that the All Blacks posted a record total against Ireland, eclipsing the 59 points scored in the second test in Wellington in 1992. But even so, Mehrtens' personal tally of 33 points, from six penalties, five conversions and a try, improved Matthew Cooper's previous highest tally against Ireland by 10 points. He even missed the final 14 minutes when Hart let Jon Preston celebrate his 30th birthday with his ninth test cap. Mehrtens also set a record for the most penalty goals against Ireland, improving his own mark by two, and in the process took his own personal tally beyond 300 test points to 319 from 19 tests. "It's nice, but something I don't worry too much about," Mehrtens said of his record-breaking achievements. "To win by 48 points is a pretty good effort and I just took advantage of that. It's probably something I'll look back on more. I got a lot of opportunities today. I got a lot of penalty attempts. I always stay as far away from (skipper) Justin Marshall as I can and not look like it's me running in to say, 'Yes, I'll take the shot'. I know the crowd boos when we kick it, so I really try and stay away if it's Justin picking the shot at goal so I'm not going to get dragged into it. I only step forward if I get called to do it. I don't want to look like I'm a glory seeker looking to kick all the points."

Mehrtens tally helped him reached the 300 points in rugby tests mark but he hadn't done it as fast as Auckland super boot Grant Fox. Fox reached 300 in 18 tests, one less than Mehrtens who passed the milestone in his 19th test. Fox was also ahead of Mehrtens at his 19th test. By then Fox had scored 320 points to Mehrtens' 319. Fox went on to amass 645 points in his 46 tests. Mehrtens did beat Fox to 100 and 200 points. Together with Southland's Simon Culhane and Auckland's Carlos Spencer, Mehrtens reached 100 in five tests, one better than Fox. Mehrtens was one better again to 200 points. He reached that milestone in 12 tests, Fox took 13.

Mehrtens would add another ten points to his test tally the following weekend in the All Blacks' 25-8 win against England at Old Trafford. Despite the win it was a scratchy effort from the All Blacks and their first five who missed touch on three occasions from penalties. Some scribes had Spencer back in the test team for the next test at Wembley against Wales. But Hart was having none of it and Mehrtens held his place and was back to something near his best in the 42-7 win. His rifled long, raking wiper kicks helped clear the All Blacks out of their 22 on numerous occasions as the All Blacks scored five tries to Wales' one.

While Cullen – who bagged three more tries against the Welsh – was stealing the headlines in the UK, Doug Golightly, writing in *The Truth*, was in no doubt who the success story of the tour – which still had one more test against England to be played – had been... He wrote: "The man exercising the control which has sparked these clinical test wins, has been Andrew Mehrtens. Remember Mehrtens had a dismal international season. Invalided out of the first test of the year, against Fiji, he had to watch Carlos Spencer slot in smoothly and even surpass all expectations as a goal-kicker. Mehrts was shut out, but the long break on the bench gave him a thirst for the game. He was jumping out of his skin for NPC rugby, even if his goal-kicking took time to come right. Ironically, that break from the international game might have rebounded favourably for Mehrtens on this tour. Spencer missed the end of Auckland's campaign because of injury, and there wasn't a great deal of doubt that Mehrts would be first-choice for the tests. Spencer hasn't had a look-in since, and patchy first and third matches didn't help his cause. Mehrtens has significant support from the man whose world record he could ultimately threaten.

"Michael Lynagh, now earning his pension with Saracens, rates Mehrtens in one word: 'Complete.' The man who spanned Mark Ella, Grant Fox, Frano Botica, Hugo Porta, Jonathan Davies, Joel Stransky... in the course of his 72-cap 911-points test career, is an unashamed Mehrtens admirer. Says 'Noddy' Lynagh: 'He is the complete international fly-half. He controls the game in an efficient and unfussy manner. Sometimes you don't even know he is there. Rare error that is real quality. While others get the plaudits, Andrew gets on with his game and makes them tick. I like that in a top-class rugby player. He very rarely makes an error, and he executes everything so well. It's nice to see a player make things look easy. You have to marvel at his ability to make breaks and put players into space.'

"Well, we know that it is part of the Mehrtens make-up, and part of his attraction. He does try things, although he does make mistakes. His first rep coach, Vance Stewart, once warned to never expect a perfect Mehrtens match, because of a youthful exuberance to explore and experiment. But the Mehrtens on this tour has had a new steel about him. Maybe it was that time on the bench, the loss of his No 10 jersey, that persuaded him to eliminate a little of the experimental attitude, to harden up, to make it impossible to take from him the pivot's jersey."

Mehrtens' teammates certainly had a lot of confidence in him. In the final test of the tour at Twickenham the forwards couldn't get rid of the ball fast enough against a rampant England pack. The All Blacks were disjointed and rudderless – the loss of Fitzpatrick finally telling on the side as they stumbled to a 26-26 draw. Mehrtens was one of the few All Blacks to come out of the game with his reputation intact. Despite missing a dropped goal three minutes from time he scored a try, landed four penalties and slotted home two conversions.

Mehrtens had – for the time being at least – seen off the challenge of Spencer. He'd ended the year as arguably the world's best No 10. And in a revealing interview with the *Sunday Star Times* he gave an insight of what it was like to live through a rivalry that had captured the imagination of the public. "I never wanted Carlos to play badly," he declared, "I always wanted the team and him to do well. I even took a lot of delight in watching him play. He's very exciting, he loves to attack, he loves using his skills and he's great to watch. I mean that sincerely."

Mehrtens admitted being a bench player had been a difficult role to play. "I was fine, but I just couldn't see what I could do to get back into the team. I got a bit nervous and started to think too much about what I should be doing, instead of just doing it. I was tentative. I started to wonder if I'd lost my confidence." He said he gained a lot of confidence from Canterbury's early NPC win against Wellington. "That gave the team a lot of confidence and it gave me a lot of confidence. It suddenly reminded me what I was in this for. I was back playing 80 minutes and it was like it all came flooding back." And, Mehrtens said, it took him a while to cope with the constant public comparisons to his arch-rival. "It does make you more aware of what they're doing, how well they're playing. I'm really aware of what Carlos is doing in provincial rugby. And it sometimes makes you start looking at yourself a bit. 'Am I measuring up?' You can tense up and it can work against you."

HAPPINESS, they say, is fleeting. Especially if it's 1998 and you are a Crusader and an All Black. The variations of highs and lows experienced by red 'n blacks that year were of the extreme kind. Ecstasy one moment. Oblivion the next. The Super 12 would provide the highest of the highs while the All Blacks would send the rugby nation crashing back to earth like never before. Indeed, it would be a year that All Blacks rugby would fail to recover from until the new millennium.

BUT before the Men In Black took centre stage (and took us to the brink) there was a Super 12 to be played. Wayne Smith had taken the Crusaders from rock bottom in 1996 and turned them into a top half side a year later. There was some hope in 1998 that semifinal football would be possible but the Blues – winners of the first two tournaments – were rightly instilled as firm favourites. And why not? Graham Henry's team included 18 All Blacks including some of the greatest of the day – Sean Fitzpatrick, Zinzan Brooke, Michael Jones, Robin Brooke, Craig Dowd, Jonah Lomu and a man-child named Carlos.

But Smith too had been busy building up his own franchise and the early indications were that real progress had been made. Weeks out of the season proper the Crusaders crunched the Blues 33-0 in Coolum, Queensland in the opening game of the Southern Cross Cup series. And while it was only a pre-season game it did at least give the Crusaders players and management the belief that they were making progress. And by the time they headed north for the opening Super 12 game against the Chiefs, confidence was high. The majority of the squad had won the NPC the previous year and while the Super 12 was a step up from that, the self-belief garnered by gaining the provincial title had stuck.

Someone however had forgotten to tell the Chiefs who won the season opening game 25-23. Mehrtens had been outplayed by his former understudy Leon MacDonald who had been moved north by John Hart who saw the former Marlborough fullback as a potential first five. Hart's thinking was that he would have limited opportunities behind Mehrtens at the Crusaders and because the Chiefs were light on No 10s the deal was done. And it paid off as MacDonald landed five penalties while an out-of-sorts Mehrtens missed five of his six shots at goal.

Jonah Lomu was just one of the All Blacks in the great Blues team in 1998.

Mehrtens sluggish start to the year continued in round two. The Crusaders achieved their biggest winning margin against the Waratahs (33-12) despite another night off with his boot by the first five-eighths who missed three penalty goal attempts as well as two second spell dropped goals. Worse news that night was the injury to halfback Justin Marshall. He ruptured his Achilles tendon and wouldn't be sighted in the Super 12 again. The news hit the team hard… as did consecutive loses over the next two weekends to the Reds (35-9) and champion Blues outfit (31-24).

The pressure was getting to Mehrtens. After the loss to the Blues he went public with stinging attack on referee Steve Walsh. "I don't know whether it's coincidence or not, but he's bad every time," Mehrtens said after the game. "I found him inconsistent tonight. I am no expert but it's obvious the touch judges aren't either. They should be a lot more accountable, these referees." The following day Mehrtens refused to retract his comments about Walsh because he had expressed his true feelings. "However, I would stress that the referee didn't lose us the game. We made bad mistakes in the first half and that's what cost us the match."

Mehrtens, while upsetting the Crusaders and NZRU management, had come to life. He trained the house down in the days leading up to the game in Christchurch against the Northern Bulls. A cheeky dropped goal in the 31-20 win gave a glimpse of the class that had so far eluded him in the opening month of the Super 12. And then, seven days later in Timaru,

Mehrtens stretched the limits at time – especially when talking about officials in the press.

he produced arguably one of the best individual performances in the history of Super rugby.

The opponents were the ACT Brumbies and the game would be won 38-26. Mehrtens had a hand in three tries and scored another himself. With his goal kicking boot back on form he had a personal tally of 18 points and was now the competition's top scorer with 78 points from six matches. His coach, Wayne Smith – who played 18 games for the All Blacks at first five between 1980 and 1985 – paid Mehrtens the ultimate compliment after the game. "I have not seen many number 10's play better than that," Smith told the thong of reporters. "He was magnificent. He was into everything, even the tackling."

The Press' Bob Schumacher captured the moment of Mehrtens' try brilliantly. "Although Mehrtens converted six of his eight goal kicking chances, he offered a lot more to the win than kicking alone," wrote the respected scribe. "Mehrtens did what William Webb Ellis did at Rugby School well over 100 years ago. He picked up the ball and ran. Whereas Ellis's actions caused gasps of horror, Mehrtens's on the run drew cries of approval."

Mehrtens said it was "about time" he got the legs pumping. "Usually the flankers run off the sides and the five-eighths has a go from second or third phases when the loosies have been committed. In the last three or four years I probably haven't done enough of that. Just being a threat myself and drawing the defence so guys can run off me gives us other options. I guess they didn't expect me to run – then neither did I! But once in the first half I passed to Reuben Thorne when I should have kept going." Mehrtens allowed himself a wee smile after scoring his own try, his third in 13 Super 12 appearances over two seasons. "I'm always surprised to score a try but it was a pleasant surprise. It was a good build-up from the guys to get us down that end."

Next up it was the Western Stormers. Mehrtens collected 22 points in a 37-25 win in Christchurch. Then the Highlanders were dispatched 40-24 at Lancaster Park with Mehrtens raking up a 25 point haul – including three dropped goals. "All three times I wasn't really expecting the ball. I didn't have time to think. That's normally when you miss, when you're doing it on pure instinct. I am just elated with the result. I was a bit worried about the game. We knew it was a sell-out and we knew there would be a lot of people cheering for Otago."

For the third successive week, Mehrtens was hailed by the opposition coach for an outstanding all-round display. Highlanders coach Tony Gilbert said Mehrtens was "absolutely magical".

Next up it was the Hurricanes in Napier. Another 24 points to Mehrtens in a 39-17 win. "His direction was wonderful," Crusaders assistant coach Peter Sloane said. "The way he works the play shows the maturity he has got into his game in the Super 12. He's more consistent and we need him to be on his game." Others were impressed too. *The Dominion's* senior sports writer Russell Gray. "While his skills and vision on the ball had been obvious on television I hadn't appreciated (Mehrtens') work off the ball. At the risk of committing heresy I compared his influence on the Crusaders to Eric Cantona's on Manchester United during their four championship wins in five years. United were virtually unbeatable when Cantona was on song. He called the tune even though there were other superbly talented players in the side. That is how I saw Mehrtens."

And this, from *The Truth's* Hedley Mortlock. "There was a priceless moment late in the Crusaders' match against the Hurricanes which showed why Andrew Mehrtens is the deadliest player in world rugby. It is frozen in memory. The Hurricanes had just scored a second try and caught the sniff of a catch-up victory. Mehrtens received good defensive, set-piece ball, summed up the entire match situation in a tick and cruelly drilled the pill 60 metres to the sideline. It was a one-man, one-touch heart-breaker, like being behind in tennis and your opponent is still waiting to destroy you with backhand passing shots. Mehrtens made a rudimentary kick into touch a weapon of mental torture. If rugby at the top level is mostly played in the mind, then his rugby IQ sometimes borders on the evil genius. And the brain under that boyish haircut has this season been cooking up even more fiendish plots to torment the Crusaders' opponents."

The Crusaders, on track for a semi-final spot after five consecutive wins boarded a flight for South Africa for games against the Golden Cats and Coastal Sharks. A win against the Cats would guarantee the Crusaders a semi final place for the first time; a win against the Cats and the Sharks would book them a home semifinal. With confidence at an all time high, with a backline brimming with the energy of Mark Mayerhofler and blockbusting power of Norm Berryman and with a pack lead by the workaholic Todd Blackadder and Mark Hammett, the Crusaders delivered two wins. The Cats were overcome 34-25 while the Sharks, who would be their semifinal opponents in Christchurch the following week, were disposed of in Durban by a 32-20 score line.

In the build up to the semi-final Sharks' skipper Gary Teichmann had said his team would target Mehrtens after he was given too much space and time in Durban. "Apparently they're after me," Mehrtens responded. "If they single me out for special treatment then it will free up other guys. The space I got last week was provided by our forwards so it is important we do that again. I don't think it puts any extra pressure on me. It's a matter of my reacting quickly and decisively and if we operate well as a team, it makes it easier for us to function as individuals." Mehrtens responded on the pitch too – kicking 16 points in his team's 36-32 win to take his tally to 196 – 26 more than the previous Super 12 record set in 1997 by Sharks fullback Gavin Lawless.

In the build up to the final against the Blues at Eden Park All Blacks coach John Hart named his trial teams. The All Blacks were playing two tests against

England before another Tri-nations series against the Wallabies and Springboks. Surprisingly Mehrtens was the only Crusader named in the shadow test team's starting line-up. Mayerhofler and Blackadder had to be content with places on the reserves bench. Fellow Crusaders Scott Robertson, Norm Maxwell, Mark Hammett, Kevin Nepia, Norm Berryman and Steve Surridge had made the opposition New Zealand 'A' side.

Some of Hart's decisions fired up certain Crusaders. With eight consecutive wins under their belts they smelt Blues blood. But it would need to be an incredible effort to go to Eden Park and beat the two-time defending champions. Yes, they were without Sean Fitzpatrick whose career was now at an end, and Jonah Lomu had failed an injury test late in the week. But the Blues had plenty to play for. They were determined to send off their Wales-bound coach Graham Henry in style. And a look at the match-ups across the park points to a win to the Blues.

The Crusaders would like to have thought their fullback Daryl Gibson had more to offer than All Black and Blues counterpart Adrian Cashmore. Things seemed even on the wing where prospective All Blacks, Joeli Vidiri and Stormin' Norman Berryman would have their big battle. Forgotten All Blacks Eroni Clarke and Tabai Matson squared off at centre while a future All Black and one from the past would meet when Mark Mayerhofler pitted his wits against Lee Stensness at second five-eighths. The two best first five-eighths in the country, Mehrtens and Spencer were set to renew a rivalry. Steve Surridge, an All Black in 1997, would clash with Zinzan Brooke's successor – the young Xavier Rush, and Scott Robertson had the chance to gain ground on the higher-rated Mark Carter. Inspirational captains Michael Jones and Todd Blackadder would go head-to-head while two of the country's most promising locks, Norm Maxwell and Royce Willis would attempt to cancel each other out. And then there was the real heat in the engine room. The Blues had world-class props Olo Brown and Craig Dowd itching to go alongside rookie rake James Christian. The Crusaders it seemed wouldn't take a backwards step however with a front row of hooker Mark Hammett and hardened props Stu Loe and Kevin Nepia.

The final was a classic. Leading by only 3-0 after having first use of a moderate south-westerly breeze and struggling against the Blues defence, the Crusaders looked as if they were well out of the running when the Blues took charge of the third quarter. For once the Crusaders' defensive pattern failed early in the second spell and Blues second five-eighth Lee Stensness weaved into the clear from broken play to put hooker James Christian across. Soon after Mehrtens failed to find touch and was punished by a long-range Adrian Cashmore dropped goal. At 10-3 ahead the Blues, now seemingly camped permanently inside the Crusaders 22, were poised to deliver the knockout blow when they mounted four attacking scrums on the Crusaders' line. Canterbury conceded a penalty and a second offence would surely have led to a penalty try from referee Paddy O'Brien. But somehow the Crusaders survived, and the siege ended when an attempt by the Blues to move wide was foiled after wing Joeli Vidiri received an unfavourable bounce from a stab kick.

It was here, in fact, that the injection of fresh legs by coaches Wayne Smith and Peter Sloane began to take its toll, with Tony Marsh in the midfield and flanker Angus Gardiner making a big impact in the game's final stages. Against the run of play, the Crusaders drew level at 10-10 when, virtually for the first time in the second spell, they broke out of their own half to rattle the Blues

ABOVE: John Hart was about to go into one of the most pressurised years of his career.
FOLLOWING PAGE: Mehrtens was back in black in 1998 – by the end of the year he'd wish he hadn't been.

defenders with fierce tackling, and lock Norm Maxwell was on hand to collect a spilled ball and scamper away for a try. An exchange of penalties by Cashmore and Mehrtens brought it to 13-13 with six minutes to go, raising visions of a fulltime stalemate and the need for another 20 minutes. But the Blues, having failed to exploit what should have been an overwhelming territorial and possession edge, began to crack. Misjudgments were made in their backline, illustrated by Lee Stensness and Carlos Spencer resorting to long-range dropped goal attempts. In the final few minutes it was the boot of Mehrtens which proved to be another decisive factor. Earlier he had made uncharacteristic errors, three times failing to find touch even from penalties, but towards fulltime he gained invaluable position with a touch finder. And then, *the moment*. He put up a last chip-kick which pressured Cashmore and Ofisa Tonu'u into fumbling and let wing James Kerr score taking the score to 20-13. The Crusaders were champions.

Mehrtens was left shaking his head at fulltime, wondering how they had snatched victory and thankful the game ended when it did. "It went by in a blur and I'm sure most of the guys felt that. It was like test match rugby and to get to the end of it is very relieving. It was just a matter of hanging in there. At times I worried we might have been losing a bit of belief in ourselves, especially when we were down on our own line. At that point I guess the team could have folded and let Auckland romp away with it." He said the Crusaders would have been out of the game if the Blues had scored again when the score was 10-3. "I guess maybe they felt the same and went off the boil and we managed to hold on to the ball a lot better in the last 20 minutes."

Mehrtens said communication was they key to the last minute try scored by Kerr. "I just reacted to a call from James. That's part of what it's been about for us. When we've performed our best as a team we've communicated well. He called the chip ahead and had

the gas to follow it up and the presence of mind to wait around in the in-goal for the ball to bobble free and dive on it. I was 40m away so I didn't really see what happened. The nasty bounce was planned…"

Within a week the hype and razzle dazzle of Super 12 rugby had been replaced with the serious stuff – the beginning of an All Blacks season. With no end of year tour – and with the World Cup only a year away – much was expected from John Hart's men. After all they hadn't been beaten in a test since the 'dead rubber' against South Africa in 1996 and despite the retirements of Frank Bunce, Sean Fitzpatrick and Zinzan Brooke confidence was high. Before the first test team of the year could be named there was the small matter of an All Blacks trial at North Harbour Stadium. Mehrtens, on a ground which had been his bogey in the last two years, slotted two sideline conversions to get that monkey off his back and he finished with 20 points, succeeding with seven of his nine goal attempts in the New Zealand Barbarians' 55-14 win against New Zealand A.

The All Blacks side to play against England in Dunedin included three players starting a test for the first time – hooker Anton Oliver, centre Mark Mayerhofler and halfback Ofisa Tonu'u. And there was a new skipper onboard – Taine Randell. For Mehrtens things couldn't have been more different than the year before. He was the undisputed No 1 and was in a relaxed mood as the team prepared in Queenstown. "Last year I was injured at the start of the Super 12 as well, but it's all gone much better this season. I've decided it's a lot more enjoyable playing rugby consistently week in, week out without getting injured so I'm not even thinking about injuries going into the test. What I am thinking about is lifting my standard, pushing myself harder, and trying to minimize mistakes. I want to play an error-free role in the team."

The under-strength English – beaten by a record 76-0 by Australia the previous week – were nothing short of a rabble. The All Blacks cruised to a 64-22 win at the 'Brook and, at Eden Park seven days later, stumbled a little as they got home 40-10. The lack of leadership in the All Blacks set up told in Auckland and with the Wallabies the next opponents in Melbourne in two weeks time there was plenty to work on – and the media let them know it. "The public and media have worked at the side mentally and I think they are pretty bruised by that," said Hart. "I don't think we'll be lacking for motivation. The heat's on, the guys know that and I won't have to say much. I think the key element is going to be the physical thing."

The Wallabies would end a seven-match losing streak to the All Blacks in emphatic fashion, outplaying their vaunted opposition 24-16 in the Tri-nations rugby opener. The decision-making of Mehrtens suffered under pressure and the woes spread into the goal kicking where he and Carlos Spencer, who replaced him in the 45th minute, missed five of their seven attempts at goal. "Too many mistakes and too many missed kicks," said a disappointed Hart immediately after the test. "There was a lack of composure in decision-making areas. We just didn't hold on to the ball long enough."

Mehrtens – who lost his perfect winning record against the Wallabies – was not blaming the new Summit ball for his woes. "The balls are more difficult to kick than the Gilbert. However, I didn't strike the ball well. I don't know why that is. The balls are hard to kick: you have to make a mental effort to get in and give it a bit more of a thump than normal because it's got no carry. Maybe that affected my timing… but I

Mehrtens would lose his winning record against the Wallabies.

didn't kick the ball well, so there's no excuses there. I doubt if it's possible to take (a winning record) through a career. If anything, the loss may take a bit of pressure off. It's obviously never good to have a loss but we have to take some positives out of it. If that takes some of the pressure off going into the South African game, and it gives us the desire to beat Australia and prove a point next time, that's got to be the positive."

Initially Hart piled the responsibility for the defeat on himself. "I take full responsibility for the performance and I take full responsibility for the selections of these players," Hart said. "What we've got here is a situation where I believe we have the best players, but we had a number coming back from injury and ideally we wouldn't have wanted them all to come back at once. We got into the position where, with the late withdrawal of Mark Mayerhofler, of being forced into playing Scott (McLeod) earlier than we might have wanted to. But what we are trying to do is build a team longer term, and at some stage we have to build these players into form. How else are they going to get the form? We believed we had the players we could win the game with, and we thought at the same time that we would be a lot better for the experience."

Within a day he had changed his tune. Andrew Mehrtens, Hart would say, was responsible for one in every three All Black errors in the loss. "He has just been a little inconsistent and maybe the error rate has been too high. When we revisit the game we are just making too many errors, and he's one of those players who have been involved in that." Hart said video analysis of the game revealed that Mehrtens's lack of direction and control was responsible for 33 percent of the All Blacks errors.

The reaction from the Canterbury province was immediate. Hart was cast as the villain. Mehrtens – the favorite son who only weeks earlier had delivered the Super 12 championship – was now being singled out by the All Blacks coach – an Aucklander – for a test loss. The anti-Hart brigade grew in numbers tenfold

overnight, and then it doubled again when Hart named his team for the Springbok's game in Wellington and Mehrtens had been replaced by Spencer in the run-on side. "It is a difficult decision, because we have two class five-eighths," Hart explained. "Ever since Carlos has come off the bench as an impact player he has played so well that it was instrumental in us making that decision. Andrew by his own admission will be a little concerned about his inconsistency in the last two tests and his high error-rate. We cannot afford those at this level. (Mehrtens) had some very good parts, some of his breaking and running, but some of the options in terms of pushing passes at the wrong time got us into trouble."

Angus Morrison, writing in Wellington's *Evening Post* summed up the mood. "John Hart is considered the man manager of all man managers, but his handling of Andrew Mehrtens' dumping was bizarre. Rather than quietly take Mehrts aside and suggest that he shouldn't have done this, should have done that and perhaps finding touch now and then would have been nice, Hart has thrown the young man to the wolves. He could have easily said he was simply rotating his first five-eighths, or that Spencer has a better record against South Africa. But no. Facing a media and a public baying for blood, Hart has thrown them Mehrtens. That's an extremely harsh call. Sure, he didn't have a great game, but Spencer didn't exactly set the MCG alight when he came on. Mehrtens seems to be paying for a poor game by his mate, Justin Marshall. And if Hart is so keen on punishing poor performances, how many more uninspiring games from the great Michael Jones do we have to put up with? And when is captain Taine Randell going to be given the No 6 jersey which so obviously suits him better than the No 8 version?"

And Phil Gifford – who was now becoming an outspoken opponent of Hart's posed this question in his *Sunday Star Times* column. "Has any All Black coach ever given so much detail about why he dropped a player as John Hart did over Andrew Mehrtens? And was Mehrtens totally responsible for exactly 33% of every error committed by the team at the MCG?"

And the former All Blacks selector Peter Thorburn added his opinion as well "You don't air your linen in public," Thorburn said. "You do not criticise your players in the media. That is the first way to destroy a person's confidence and those sort of things should never happen. All that does is hang a guy up to dry and then the other people (players) are thinking 'when's my turn coming'. That is fear-coaching."

The country was divided and the All Blacks played like they knew it as they went down at Athletic Park 13-3. The All Blacks had played two tests in the competition and the Tri-nations title was already gone. Spencer had offered nothing to the back line and Mehrtens was put on in the 49th minute. Indeed, he was responsible for the only score for the New Zealanders when he slotted home a penalty. "Hart's decision to pick Spencer ahead of Mehrtens backfired," wrote Campbell Mitchell in the *Sunday News*. "In fact, the decision to axe Mehrtens after the loss to Australia single-handedly lost the All Blacks the test. Spencer wasn't up to the job. He missed five penalty attempts and his tactical kicking and option-taking was poor. By the time Mehrtens took the field with 31 minutes to play, it was too late."

Hart took the blame. "The decision to play Spencer was wrong because he didn't kick the goals and whoever was there had to kick the goals". "We've now kicked three goals out of 13 – and that includes Andrew – in the last two tests and that's a clear expression of where we're at. In hindsight, the decision to play Carlos was wrong, but I stand by it and it was proven to be wrong because we didn't kick the goals. Three out of 13 is a frightening rate. I'm not ducking responsibility – I'm accountable. We're going through some difficult times, but it's only our third loss in 26 tests."

Hart put Mehrtens straight back into the team for the Christchurch test against the Wallabies. But, as anyone who was watching this All Blacks team knew, the problems facing Hart were much deeper than who should wear the No 10 jersey. So it was no surprise that the Bledisloe Cup was lost when the Wallabies won 27-23. The All Blacks two late tries gave Mehrtens some confidence as the team faced a road trip to Durban and Sydney. "There's no reason why we can't go in firing like that in the next game against the Springboks. That's something we've got to work towards. I thought we'd reset this last week and got a bit more relaxation and enjoyment into it, rather than the stress which has punctuated the last month. It didn't quite work, but we're not far off. The mindset is certainly more positive than it has been the last two games. We've done everything we can. The more we play as a team the better those combinations and 50-50 plays will come off. We've got to just work on being aggressive and stringing so many phases together until they're so low on men that it's inevitable we score. We made vital mistakes that put our forwards under pressure."

But this was not a happy time in New Zealand rugby. Three consecutive test loses had former All Blacks coming out of the woodwork. Stu Wilson, the former wing, took aim at Mehrtens. "I've never been keen to 'bag' individual All Blacks but I've been singularly unimpressed with the efforts of Andrew Mehrtens and Walter Little. I realise there's some extenuating circumstances, like the lack of aggression from the pack and the speed of the ball from halfback but their combined efforts have been average. In fact, Mehrtens' performance at Jade Stadium, especially his tactical kicking, was appalling. Ever since the international season kicked off we've seen a real Jekyll and Hyde side to the Canterbury first five, when you compare him to his Super 12 performances. He's gone from being a dominant match winner to being an ineffective, skittery player, who's apparently lost his composure. To be honest I can't understand how that can happen other than to state that perhaps he finds it difficult making the step up to the big time."

"Justin and I are pretty close and it's disappointing when that happens to your mate. I was surprised, but I can't really comment on selections. It's not up to me. But maybe it should be? I'm sure guys like Fitzy and Zinny have been involved in discussions on selection issues before. I've never really considered it, but ... as a first-five, especially having been around for four or five years, maybe it's part of my job to get involved in those sorts of discussions."

Mehrtens was the one asking the questions after the test at Kings Park. The All Blacks were stunned before despair started sinking in after their single point loss to South Africa in the Tri-Nations rugby test in Durban. The All Blacks dominated the game for 65 minutes only to score two tries to South Africa's four, three of which came in the last 15 minutes with the winner being scored by hooker James Dalton in injury time to deliver a 24-23 victory. "Whatever happened there? How did we lose this one?" Mehrtens said. "Everyone's just stunned. I know we'll be absolutely gutted."

By the time the All Blacks arrived in Sydney for the last test of the season there was very little belief they could turn things around. And so it proved. Predictably the team succumbed to the Wallabies 19-14, the All Blacks' fifth consecutive loss. It was, and still is, New Zealand rugby's worst international year since 1949.

Within hours of the game Hart and Mehrtens were publicly at odds over the tactics employed. Hart was critical of Mehrtens' decision to kick away the ball too much when New Zealand was struggling for possession, describing many kicks as "aimless". Hart suggested Mehrtens' over-kicking was against the All Black plan. "I can't defend that actually," Hart said when asked whether Mehrtens kicked more than intended. "That's the one sad thing for me, some of the kicking was just not in our plan."

Mehrtens insisted kicking was the best option. "We were kicking the ball away because we were struggling for field position. Whenever we had the ball it seemed they had more defenders than we had

ABOVE: Mehrtens – and the rest of the All Blacks – felt like mugs after they lost in Durban.
PAGE 81: Mehrtens kept his head down while controversy stirred all around him.

attackers, and you can't play with the ball in hand if you've got more defenders than attackers. The kicks behind were on. Sometimes I was trying to kick to a certain place but miskicked. Other than that, I maintain it was the right thing to do."

Mehrtens admitted Hart's criticism of his kicking game in Sydney was "a wee bit" hard to handle, but he says he is still enjoying All Black rugby and wanted to be part of a World Cup year revival. "In general, New Zealand was right behind (the All Blacks). But you know there are always going to be some negative comments… and factions who want this guy out and this one in. But it does (hurt) a wee bit when I really hadn't had a chance to discuss things with him. But if John Hart thinks I am not the right one to read the game or make decisions like that, then I am answerable to him and I won't start in games." Mehrtens maintained, however, that it was his execution rather than his option-taking which was awry on occasions. "I guess the biggest concern going into next year for the All Blacks is that we haven't been able to dominate possession or control it as much as we have been used to in the past. Nobody is crowing. But the feeling is as good as can be expected after you've had five losses in a row and been told you're the worst test team since 1949. The guys all get on fine. There's no bitching… we've had fun during the week and we've certainly put in the hard work and haven't shirked anything. We've done everything but win. It's obviously disappointing, but we're in it together and adversity often brings a team together. Obviously, with the results, it's hard to enjoy yourself as much as we did last year, for example, but I'm still enjoying it."

JOHN Hart survived the summer. Laurie Mains took a call from NZRU board member Kevin Roberts who offered him the coaching reigns but the Otago stalwart declined. So Hart – part of the unsuccessful coaching team

at the 1991 World Cup – would get his second chance at rugby's Holy Grail. But while Hart survived the summer All Blacks Jonah Lomu, Joeli Vidiri and Isitolo Maka didn't. They were omitted from the summer training squad camp at the Hobsonville RNZAF Base after they "did not meet certain fitness standards". It wasn't the most positive start to a World Cup year…

ANDREW Mehrtens certainly hadn't had a summer off. He'd hit the gym after Canterbury's NPC semifinal exit. In 1998 he tipped the scales at 77kg and he was now sitting at 82kg. His major motivation was to increase his confidence in defensive situations. "If you get an opportunity to run at Mark Mayerhofler or run at me, most people would pick me. I just don't want to be a weaker link in the chain than any of the others. There's been a bit of talk about (Stephen) Larkham (Australia) and Henry Honiball (South Africa) being bigger guys and you start considering yourself a bit of a lightweight. There are some aspects of my attacking game I want to work on, but I just thought 'first things first'. If you don't look like you mean business, people are more likely to have a crack at you."

There were plenty of people lining up to have a crack at Mehrtens after the Crusaders' round eight Super 12 win against the Northern Bulls in Pretoria. The Crusaders had lost their previous two games to the Highlanders and Stormers and a win was in desperate need for the defending champions. So when Mehrtens was successful with a late dropped goal that gave them a 30-28 win emotions were high. And so was Mehrtens' middle finger – a finger he raised to sections of the Loftus Versfeld Stadium crowd. "It was just a spur of the moment response. I know it sounds funny but I didn't mean any disrespect by it. I suppose I let myself down and I apologise for it," he said. "I guess all I wanted to say (to the crowd) was 'tough luck, you tried to put me off but it didn't work'. It was aimed for some of the poorer sections of the crowd that were laughing and jeering. I didn't mean it to be directed at Northern Transvaal people in general."

NZRU chief executive David Moffett asked Canterbury Rugby Football Union chief Steve Tew to file a report on the incident. Moffett said he would rather the incident had not happened. "I suggest that Andrew might take that point of view too, seeing as he has already apologised. Tew said Mehrtens should not have let the crowd get to him. A professional has to put that to the back of his mind. But he was given a hard time apparently, and it was pretty personal."

Moffett would eventually refuse to divulge what action, if any, the union saw fit to take against Mehrtens. "Andrew apologised and acknowledged his mistake both immediately after the incident and on a number of occasions since then. He is genuinely sorry for his behavior and the NZRU have taken that into account," Moffett said in a statement. "While it is board policy not to comment on player contractual matters, we can say that Andrew agrees that the process and outcomes in this matter are commensurate with the incident."

The Truth's Doug Golightly, not always in Mehrtens' camp when it came to his rivalry with Carlos Spencer, was adamant which side of finger-gate he was on. "Mehrtens, and the Crusaders, do a hell of a lot in the role model stakes off-the-field," he wrote. "In fact, I've witnessed first hand just how dedicated Mehrtens is to the young people who idolise him. He never turns away an autograph seeker and he always has a cheery word for the fans. Add to that the fact he hasn't blotted his copybook off the field and you've got a popular and likeable rugby star. Those are the blokes we should treasure rather than knock down. And surely we don't want blokes like Mehrts to turn into cold, unemotional robots on-the-field. The bloke has been unfairly bagged and perhaps he should have given another two finger salute to all those who stuck it up him."

Mehrtens responded by letting his boot instead of his fingers do the talking in the Crusaders' 58-38 rugby win against the Cats the following weekend. He scored the perfect 10 from 10 as he contributed 23 points at Nelson's Trafalgar Park. The Crusaders' revival continued through the end of the round-robin with a 34-29 win against the Sharks followed by a 38-22 win in Sydney. "This win shows the measure of the character of the team," coach Wayne Smith said. "We've got the momentum going now. A lot of that has been through Andrew Mehrtens. He's hitting something like 84% with his goal kicking and that's phenomenal. But he's playing really well too – he and Justin Marshall have clicked." The Crusaders were in the play-offs again – although this time home advantage had been missed. To go back-to-back they would have to win their second title on the road.

Their semifinal would be against the Reds at Ballymore. Tries by Greg Feek, Caleb Ralph, Leon MacDonald and Scott Robertson helped get them home 28-22 and Smith again raved about his inside back pairing. "I'm really rapt to have them," said Smith. "They're just playing great rugby. But they're getting good ball. The tight five are getting their bodies down and smashing forward and getting some good ball. But they're using it brilliantly. They're doing their homework working hard off the field. It's just great to see them performing."

The final was to be played at Carisbrook. And with the Highlanders having to travel from Cape Town after their 33-18 win against the Stormers, the Crusaders went into the game as favourites. And they delivered on that tag with a hard-fought 24-19 win. After lifting the trophy skipper Todd Blackadder agreed the turning point of the season was Mehrtens' now infamous last-minute dropped goal to beat the Northern Bulls at Pretoria last month. "It really threw us a lifeline. That's what kept us in this competition. If we'd lost that game we probably would have been sunk. We'd have been nudged out (on points) even if we had won all our (remaining) games."

Not surprisingly it didn't take long for the focus to turn from the Super 12 to the All Blacks. The World Cup was now only five months away and the first test of the season, against Samoa at North Harbour, less than three weeks. And that was bad news for Mehrtens who had aggravated a groin injury in the final. "He had the injury before the game, he will see a surgeon in Auckland in the next 48 hours," an annoyed John Hart said. "It's quite devastating in terms of our preparation but it will give someone else another chance – and we've got to move on. I'm still hoping it won't require surgery, but we won't know that for a while. We are now having a major rethink, but we can't make any decision on that till we know the outcome of the medical review."

Tony Brown, the Highlanders first five, had emerged as the No 2 first five after his stellar Super 12 season. Carlos Spencer had failed to shine for the Blues who'd finished ninth with just four wins from their 11 games. As it turned out Mehrtens didn't need surgery on his injury and Hart's relief suggested he saw the Cantabrian as being his out and out No 1. "I had a sick feeling (when I heard he was I injured) because I think he's a very important player," Hart said. "But at the same time we won't take any risks. If he needs an operation then we'll do whatever he needs to get right because he is a key player for the World Cup. We're not going to take risks short-term."

Brown got the start against New Zealand 'A' at Dunedin – a game the All Blacks won unconvincingly 22-11. In a sign of things to come Hart had Christian Cullen – the best fullback in world rugby – playing on

An injured Mehrtens starred for the Crusaders but his injury put the All Blacks on the back foot.

the wing to allow Jeff Wilson to wear the No 15 jersey. The same formation would take the field against Samoa, again with Brown at first five and Spencer on the bench. Brown would see out the 80 minutes, kicking seven conversions and four penalties in a 71-13 win.

But there was little doubt Mehrtens would be rushed back into the test side once he was fit. And with the French due at Athletic Park for a one-off test Hart moved quickly to reinstall Mehrtens to the No 10 jersey. And the player, in the lead up to his first test against the French, told the *New Zealand Herald's* Wynne Gray he'd made some adjustments from his last test season. "At times last year my communication was down," he revealed. "A big part of playing first five-eighths is to communicate well, especially after I've had four or five weeks off with this injury. Sometimes in the past when I have not been confident then I can go a bit flat. I am aware of that and need to be talking lots to make sure our play is accurate.

"It is all about reacting well too, something we did not do last year, so we will probably not go in with too many preconceived ideas for this test."

Mehrtens found his test feet quickly. He was subbed off late in the 54-7 win – the last at Athletic Park and the last in the famous Canterbury New Zealand jersey – after suffering from cramp but he'd had a strong game, creating space for the midfield and taking the right options with and into the wind. He quickly re-established lethal combinations with Crusaders teammates Justin Marshall at halfback and Daryl Gibson at second-five and snubbed out any hope Brown or Spencer had of challenging his place in the Tri-nations tests.

He was named for the test against the 'Boks at Carisbrook and immediately declared the Springboks as New Zealand's hardest rugby opponent. "They're the toughest team to play by far because they're so physical. They're always in your face, but they're such a good team to beat because you know you've been

through a hard game to have beaten them." After the experiences of 1998 – and the five consecutive test loses – a win in the first Tri-nations game was imperative. "Not only would it be good for the confidence, but it would give us a good start to the Tri-nations series which we want to win. To do that you have to win your home games. We're targeting our home games and fortunately our first two games are at home so it has not been hard to get motivated. If those first two games go well for us we can give it a real crack when we go overseas."

Hart's All Blacks responded with a 28-0 win, in the first Adidas test match. Christian Cullen, Jeff Wilson and Justin Marshall got the tries as they blanked the 'Boks. "There will be confidence now," Mehrtens said of the World Cup year. "It's been a difficult two weeks in that we were going into the unknown as to how we would compete against South Africa. We knew they would be a lot harder physically than anything we'd encountered this year. There was some apprehension inside the team so to come through with a 28-0 score gives us confidence. It's good to be on a high and we hope to scale greater heights. At this time of the year I'd give us 8.5, maybe nine, but good won't be good enough to win the World Cup so we want to be getting to 9.5, maybe even 10 to win the World Cup. You're not going to play the perfect game but it was pretty good. We can be fairly satisfied but we have to be aware that it doesn't really happen that often."

Next up were the Wallabies at Eden Park – the team that had wiped the All Blacks' 3-0 the previous year. "We'll see how long 12 months is. We may not have made too many steps if we get knocked back down again this week. I think we would have the confidence in the squad to handle a knockdown a lot better than maybe we did last year, as a group. We lost 3-0 to them last year. It would certainly be nice to make that 3-1. They've got a lot of confidence against the All Blacks now, whereas I think the All Blacks used to be a nemesis team for them. They're a very dangerous team, they're a good thinking team, they're a very skilful team. For our own confidence, obviously it'd be another step up to put in a good performance against them.

"I don't think there's as much criticism of the team this year (from the press and public). In the last couple of years, even if the guys are confident, criticism by the media and stuff like that, of individual players, which says they're struggling for form, affects the team as a whole because you're going out thinking 'so-and-so' needs a big game to get back at his critics and stuff like that. You're sort of hoping that he does do it, but you're worrying about other guys, and it undermines your confidence. We're very determined this year. I know I'm more determined to use myself as a threat. I think that can help the team a lot, when the first five isn't tentative. I was pretty disappointed in my performances against them last year. I had been trying things. My goal-kicking was more disappointing than my general play. Even though I threw a couple of passes that got intercepted, I'd like to think that I was at least trying things. I'm the same player. I don't think a lot has changed, other than maybe I'm confident. I know I've improved in the last two or three years. [But] I'm still missing too many tackles, probably when I go too high on guys. My strength has improved, but everyone else's has, too…"

In the build up to the Bledisloe Cup Mehrtens decided to take on the media. He told the *Evening Post* some members of the New Zealand sports media were inaccurate and lacked objectivity. A "couple" had personal agendas, and said he was considering writing a book to "have a crack" back. "I think a lot of our rugby media… without being too specific… struggle to be objective. I find a lot of them… no, I won't go any further than that." But he did. "There's just a lot things that I would say are inaccurate. And it's just pretty annoying when you read things about the game and think 'well, this guy's saying that, and that's not really what it was like at all'. It tends to be when one person latches on to something, whether it's accurate or inaccurate, and labels a game, saying you had a shocker. It tends to become gospel… they don't look at it and ask 'did he really have a shocker?'" Mehrtens said the All Blacks might, in some ways, be the authors of their own negative press. "We can help that, I guess, by being a little more explanatory in what we say during the week, rather than going with the standard lead-up-to-the-game bullshit that we go through. But you don't want to give another team any ammunition. I don't expect to have all the media loving you all the time… because it's not going to happen. Same with people – you're never going to please all the people all the time. You've just got to get used to that and get a thick skin. I've never really wanted to (write a book), but I might have to have a crack at a couple of guys that I find have a crack at me on less-than-rugby issues. Some of the comments you hear are quite personal, and they don't know me."

Mehrtens was fired up – and thank goodness. In the resulting 34-15 win against the Australians he kicked 10 from 10, including a world record nine penalties. He also notched up his 100th point against Australia, his 500th point for the All Blacks and kicked a 29-point haul. "I'm not sort of aware of those sort of things," he said of his nine penalties which equaled the world mark of nine set by Japan's Keiji Hirose. "I pride myself on doing my job for the team. I wouldn't say it's ever an easy job in a test match, but certainly I've had harder kicking nights. It's sort of a shame I suppose. It's a bit of an indictment on a team when there are nine penalties all within what I would say was easily goalable range. There were none of them too far out and too difficult. We've got to be happy that we created opportunities, but maybe just being half a metre off the breakdown when we broke through meant that they were able to infringe. We'd rather be scoring five points than three but if they're going to infringe that many times, then nine lots of three is a lot of points. Twenty-seven in fact. A few of the crowd were starting to get a bit anti it as well. I told Christian Cullen after about the second to last one that he should take the next one because I didn't want to get booed. But we're in it to win the match and to take any points we can. We did win the match and we're happy about it. I think it was the most complete effort of the year. They were the tightest team we've played against. The Aussies will improve a lot but I'd like to think we can as well."

One team struggling at the time was the Springboks. Coach Nick Mallett made eight changed to his line-up for the test against the All Blacks at Pretoria. Yes, Mehrtens was back in front of the fans he'd delivered his famous gesture too. And by the end of the 80 minutes, they wished he hadn't been. After the All Blacks took a fierce battering early, they slowly forced the home side into errors before Mehrtens punished them with his diagonal tactical kicks. He was also successful with seven penalty goals while Christian Cullen – who was switched into the centre position after an injury to Darryl Gibson in the 35th minute – grabbed two tries. "His (Mehrtens') kicking was the key, he was outstanding," Mallett said. "That's the second time he's controlled and kicked New Zealand to victory. He did it against Australia as well a couple of weeks ago."

Mehrtens would have the chance to do it to the Aussies again two weeks later. The last test before the World Cup was set for the new Olympic Stadium in Sydney. And with Rod Kafer in at No 10 for the injured Stephen Larkham, the All Blacks smelt blood. With the first test having already been won in Auckland the

Mehrtens was hailed as the difference between the teams by 'Boks coach Nick Mallet.

prospect of getting the Bledisloe Cup in the bag before the World Cup was a very real one… until the kick-off. The All Blacks struggled against the Wallabies' defence patterns and managed only one try – to Mehrtens – in the 28-7 pounding. It was Mehrtens' worst performance of the international season as he wavered from his percentage game and under pressure from a rampant Australian defence couldn't get his side into any sort of field position. "Some of the things (he did) weren't in our game plan but, in saying that, the players do have a license to try things if they are on. That's the way we play," said Hart who subbed Mehrtens as one of five changes in the second spell.

Mehrtens said the All Blacks "were out-passioned" and outplayed. "We've got to take as many things as we can out of the game, but there were not a lot of positives. But we've got to learn from the experience. It is never good to lose, but it's an opportunity to learn the hard way. We got out-passioned and outplayed in probably every facet, so it wasn't enjoyable. We've got a huge amount of things to work on but what we played tonight was probably two or three steps below what we've been playing so we know we are capable of getting back up there. I certainly don't think we have shown our hand or put in a really good 80-minute performance yet. The last year in a perverse way has been good for the team… we are much better now at operating under (the) pressure that comes from the New Zealand public's desire to win every game."

When it came time for the All Blacks to head to England for the World Cup the rugby nation had

Mehrtens and Lomu – two key players for the All Blacks at the 1999 World Cup.

righted itself after the loss in Sydney and generally there was a lot of confidence around that this team would be the first All Blacks side to lift the Cup since 1987. The last time Mehrtens left for a World Cup he was a one-test rookie. On this occasion he had 34 games at the highest level of rugby under his belt and felt far more at ease about dealing with the demands. "I am much more aware about what goes on and that helps. In 1995 it was my first year playing for the All Blacks and I was very wide-eyed. There was a huge buzz about everything. Now it is more of a pinnacle, it has been a long time between World Cups. Pressure doesn't affect me more than anyone else, there's pressure on anyone. I'm the goal-kicker, the points-scorer, but then a lot of people say the game's won up front, so who knows? The guys all know the pressure's there. From everyone. It's fairly easy to sit up in the stand – I do it myself – and say, 'No, do this – not that!'"

Mehrtens said the failure to finish the job 1995 was not a motivation factor this time around.

"We want to win it for this year's sake. To win this World Cup would not make up for losing the last World Cup. Everyone that was there, or watched, would feel that it was an opportunity we missed. The guys that were there understand how bad it was to miss an opportunity like that and don't want to miss an opportunity like that again. We've got this one fantastic chance, and the guys want to make sure that we've learnt from that experience."

The first game at the 1999 World Cup would be against Tonga, then England and Italy before the knock-off phase. The main feature of the team was the return of Jonah Lomu to the left wing. That meant Tana Umaga was on the right wing. And with Wilson at fullback Christian Cullen was in the unfamiliar role of centre. By the end of the tournament it would be judged – depending on results – as either a bold or foolish move by Hart.

The game against Tonga was unconvincing. The 45-9 scoreline hints at 20 minutes of quality and 60 minutes of concern. Lomu grabbed a couple of tries while Josh Kronfeld, Byron Kelleher and Norm Maxwell also crossed the line. The back row though – Kronfeld, Taine Randell and Reuben Thorne lack cohesion as did the backline, not surprisingly. And the news got worse for the team the day following the test when Carlos Spencer wrenched his knee and was out of the tournament. Spencer was behind Mehrtens and Tony Brown in the first-five stakes but his ability to cover numerous positions in the backline meant his premature departure for Auckland was a body blow to the team.

As the next game, against England at Twickenham approached, the All Blacks management were at pains to downplay the significance of the result. While it was the coming together of two rugby superpowers, it was after all just a pool game. It was not do or die. But Mehrtens was doing everything he could to get under the skin of the England fans prior to kickoff. He told reporters he hoped the Twickenham crowd would be giving him "hell". He said he thrived on abuse. "I'm like that and I hope the Twickenham crowd gives me hell," he said. "I find it preferable to kick with a lot of noise and booing and hissing than to kick with dead silence. Most kickers say that they enjoy the atmosphere so they can transform that feeling into concentration for the kick. I don't want a sporting crowd when I'm kicking. I can't bear the silence."

Mehrtens wouldn't have minded the silence that descended over Twickeham at the end of the game. The All Blacks – with Jonah Lomu back to his best – had won 30-16. It was a win built on defence and that gave the team great confidence. Firepower was never going to be a problem for this team. So to master the art of defending your line under great pressure was a giant leap forward for Hart's team.

With the All Blacks hopelessly outclassing Italy 101-3 in its final group game attention quickly turned to the quarterfinal against Scotland at Murrayfield. Shoddy lineout work (read: Anton Oliver) and an injury to Mehrtens marred the All Blacks' 30-18 win. Mehrtens was limping late in the first half and didn't return to the field after halftime. Hart did his best to put a positive spin on the average performance. "We've got to keep everything in perspective," he said. "We had an outstanding 40 minutes – we played really well. We lost the guy (Mehrtens) who was commanding the game, at halftime. (In the second half) we tried to be too adventurous and keep the game and the momentum going when the ball was getting more and more difficult to handle. We weren't patient enough and made a lot of mistakes. We were trying to do too much. When we get into the attacking zone, we've got to be more ruthless about our execution. And maybe simpler, rather than complicated…"

With Mehrtens' knee bruised, Hart was ready to wait until the morning of the semifinal against France before making a final call on his fitness. "If you look at where he was at the time of the knock to now, it's improving all the time so that's a positive sign," Hart said three days out of the semi. "But we are still a long way from saying he is playing on Sunday. It just depends how quickly it recovers. We will wait as long as we have to and he will only play if he is right."

A day out of the game at Twickenham Mehrtens was passed fit. "He came through training… he will start," Hart announced. "He goal-kicked, he place-kicked, he punted, he got tackled, he tackled, he ran… he did everything. You couldn't get a more physical test." Mehrtens, incredibly, would line up in the semifinal outside Byron Kelleher, whose only previous test start had come against the Italians. Hart had decided the All Blacks needed to change things up and Justin Marshall was sacrificed. The invaluable Crusaders connection at the inside-backs, torn apart for the biggest game of this four-year cycle. It was a big call and one that, amongst others (Christian Cullen to centre, Jeff Wilson to fullback, Reuben Thorne to six) would ultimately prove fatal.

The French fully deserved their 43-31 win and, despite reliable kicking from Mehrtens and two thundering tries by Jonah Lomu, the French were the better side. They were justly given a standing ovation by the crowd of 70,000. French first five Christophe Lamaison, who scored 28 of his side's points, played an inspirational game with his kicking and particularly his running as he carved his way through the normally impenetrable defence of the likes of Jeff Wilson and Mehrtens. At 24-10 up, six minutes into the second half, the All Blacks were cruising. Unfortunately, they couldn't get out of cruise mode and France put on an incredible 33 unanswered points before a consolation Wilson try in the dying seconds. New Zealand was a red-hot favourite and had the benefit of a 20-9 penalty count from Scottish referee Jim Fleming, but was simply outplayed. The All Blacks were out-tackled and out-thought by a passionate French team on its way to the greatest win in its rugby history. The Tricolores would now head triumphantly to Cardiff to play Australia in the final. The All Blacks would head to the same city, but only to play a third-place playoff against South Africa – a game which also would be lost 22-18.

In the aftermath Mehrtens, who would be named winner of the K.R. Tremain Memorial Trophy for the Rugby Personality of the Year on his return from the World Cup, watched on as Hart resigned and the debate about who should replace him developed. Mehrtens publicly backed his Crusaders coach Wayne Smith who doubled as an assistant All Blacks coach. "The worrying thing is I've got a whiff of a rumour that they may decide they want a wholesale clear-out. It would be erroneous to ditch Smithy based on the last two years of All Black performances. That would be a big mistake. He wasn't as hands-on as people think, or he probably would have liked. I just hope they keep an open mind and make a decision, based on results. If they do, then they can't go past him after two Super 12 titles with the Crusaders. It would be a travesty to waste Smith's experience."

While Mehrtens' outspokenness is often admired, the reality is when he should have spoken out… he didn't. He was adamant, in hindsight, he should have spoken out when Justin Marshall was benched for the semi against the French. "Justin and I are pretty close and it's disappointing when that happens to your mate. I was surprised, but I can't really comment on selections. It's not up to me. But maybe it should be? I'm sure guys like Fitzy (Sean Fitzpatrick) and Zinny (Brooke) have been involved in discussions on selection issues before. I've never really considered it, but … as a first five, especially having been around for four or five years, maybe it's part of my job to get involved in those sorts of discussions."

Mehrtens surprised many by ending the millennium by sticking up for Hart. He told the *Press* said the blame for the All Black loss to France could not be laid at coach John Hart's door. "He's not the one who missed a tackle or let the French forwards run around him and get over the advantage line." Mehrtens said people had always assumed he and Hart didn't get on well. "But we got on fine. That hasn't been a problem. It's not as if we don't acknowledge each other."

John Hart's tenure ended in embarrassing defeat.

THE GOOD, BAD
AND DOWNRIGHT UNFAIR

HE was primed for one more shot at rugby's Holy Grail. But a coach by the name of John Mitchell – and his assistant Robbie Deans – put an end to Andrew Mehrtens' dream farewell to All Blacks rugby. But rather than fade away into rugby's distant memories, he went on to regain his All Black position before cashing in and spreading the rugby gospel to audiences in England and France.

ROBBIE Deans – the great Canterbury fullback and kicking machine – would be a pivotal figure in the life and times of Andrew Mehrtens post the 1999 World Cup. Deans, of course, had already been on hand to assist Mehrtens as Canterbury's NPC coach and Super 12 manager. But by 2000 Deans had the top coaching job at the Crusaders after Wayne Smith's elevation to the All Blacks post. And the relationship between Deans and Mehrtens would be tested many times in the next few years. Indeed, some critics had the pair at each others throats – convinced that there was a real dislike for one to the other. That, of course, was nonsense dreamt up by a media and driven by 'insiders' that never existed. Yes, the relationship was strained at times, but ultimately there was too much respect for the other's careers for the tension to be everlasting.

Their initial relationship as coach and player was a good one. When Mehrtens passed Deans as Canterbury's all-time record points scorer early in 2000 there was no gloating from Mehrtens and no melancholy from Deans. Mehrtens, with a 12-point haul in the Super 12 round three win against the Reds at Ballymore advanced his total to 2075, moving two points ahead of Deans. Mehrtens overtook two Canterbury legends that night – Fergie McCormick (2065) and Deans (2073). The player described the record as "irrelevant" while the coach sung his charge's praises. "Mehrts has made a significant contribution to Canterbury rugby in recent times and I hope it doesn't finish there. The sooner he gets to 3000 the better. He is a guy of exceptional ability and, while it is something possibly not recognised, he has already shown a fair amount of resilience in spending as long as he has in accumulating those points."

Mehrtens' resilience was tested in the Super 12 after he picked up a rib injury against the Bulls in the ninth round. He would miss the final round robin games against the Waratahs and Brumbies before earning his spot in the home semifinal against the Highlanders at Jade Stadium. The Crusaders – going for an unprecedented three-peat had cruised through the round robin. They won their opening five games before some individual brilliance from Christian Cullen stole their thunder in Wellington. And there was a glitch against the Sharks in Durban before wins against the Cats, Bulls, Waratahs and Brumbies ensured they were on another winning run going into the playoffs.

The game would pit Mehrtens against Tony Brown. The Highlanders first five – Mehrtens' understudy at the World Cup the previous year – had come on in leaps and bounds in 2000 and was now a genuine threat to the Cantabrian's hold on the All Blacks jersey. And the pressure came on Mehrtens when Justin Marshall – his trusty halfback – cried out of the game with a calf muscle injury 24 hours out of the semifinal. When Norm Maxwell was added to the injured list and news leaked that Mehrtens' rib injury was now complicated by a back injury, Crusaders fans began to lose confidence.

But Mehrtens did what he did numerous times before and played the role of hero to perfection. He banged over six penalties and two conversions for a match haul of 22 points in the 37-13 win. And, more importantly, he controlled the tempo of the match, never allowing the Highlanders to camp out in the Crusaders' 22. His long punts made sure of that. "Mehrts is a real ignition for the team," Deans said. "The players enjoy playing with him. They get excited. He's such a dominant personality on the field that it does rub off when he plays with such confidence. He was just so confident with everything he attempted out there today – he's a real class act."

Crusaders skipper Todd Blackadder – who led an impressive forwards pack on the night – didn't mind shining the spotlight on his five-eighth either, paying tribute to the lift he was able to provide with his control and huge kicking game. "It's a great feeling," he said about the territory Mehrtens was able to gain. "He's just a great player and it's a great feeling trudging up there after one of them kicks." Even the Highlanders

"The record doesn't enter my head… I'm aware of it, probably more than I let on, because you take a pride in your performance. But I think things like that are something you'll look back on when you stop playing rugby and just take a certain amount of satisfaction in. But what's important to me this weekend is winning the match. That's being completely honest – I would feel I was letting the team or the country down if I was thinking about something personal."

were acknowledging the brilliance of the All Black No 10. "Mehrts in some ways was the telling factor," Josh Kronfeld told the *Sunday Star Times*. "Andrew always seems to know when to kick and when to pass. He's just such a class player."

The win, and the Brumbies' 28-5 win against the Cats, meant the Crusaders would need to win in Canberra to make history as the first three-time winners of the competition. And they would have to do it without Marshall and their No 2 halfback Aaron Flynn. Both were injured and out of the final so Mehrtens, for the second week in a row, would play outside the inexperienced former NZ Colt, Ben Hurst. And the two of them were up against the best one-two punch in world rugby – the Wallabies' 1999 World Cup winning inside backs combo of George Gregan and Stephen Larkham.

But it was a case of "bugger the pundits" as Mehrtens emerged as the hero once again as he landed a 76th minute penalty to help deliver the Crusaders the 20-19 triumph. The Brumbies nearly snatched their first title with a frenzied second half effort and when Stirling Mortlock put his side ahead 19-17 in the 74th minute it looked like they would become the first non-New Zealand side to win the Super 12. But then up stepped Mehrtens, battling cramp, to land the testing kick, 42 metres into the breeze. "If you've got to kick one of those, he's the man to do it isn't he?" said Deans. "He was on his way off the field. He was cramping up. He was in a lot of pain. It was a remarkable piece of concentration for him to convert that into points before he departed."

Mehrtens, typically, played down his role in the victory. "I'm glad because I thought I was going to pull up pretty lame after the kick and in the end I can't remember if I did because I was watching it quite closely," Mehrtens said. "It was straight in front, but I was a wee bit nervous. In hindsight it was important but our defence over the whole game was more important than one or two kicks. They missed a few

kicks and no doubt people will say that's where we won the game." The Brumbies captain, Brett Robinson, said his heart dropped when Mehrtens lined up the last kick. "It was a bit of deja vu. Last year Mehrtens made the difference when they beat us here. He kicked a field goal from 45m and penalty goals from everywhere. He's just a magnificent goalkicker and there's only so much you can do when you are against a guy who kicks like that."

The Truth's sports editor Doug Golightly was adamant that kick alone should kill off flak from all those who liked to opine that Mehrtens – with the 1995 World Cup still on their minds – was a chocker. "It's no surprise that Mehrtens was the first five of the competition," he wrote. "For the last three years he has been one of the key players for the Crusaders dictating play, kicking goals and running the Red 'n Black cutter with all the astute awareness you'd expect from a consummate professional. At Bruce Stadium in the thrilling, nail-biting final, Mehrtens was simply outstanding. The pressure didn't faze him and he showed why he's considered to have one of the game's best big match temperaments. And it laid to rest the myth that Mehrtens is a chocker. His track record in a hellishly good career suggests otherwise. He's clearly the best first five we've got and now that Carlos Spencer doesn't seem to feature in the All Blacks plans, it's a case of Mehrts first, daylight second. There's no question the 39-test veteran holds the key to All Black success but he has to be given the protection he needs. That means the All Black loose forwards must take an uncompromising approach. If they win him some space and time, then

ABOVE: Mehrtens' late goal against the Brumbies delivered a famous victory.
PAGE 92: Mehrtens kicks for touch on tour in the Northern Hemisphere in 2002.
PAGE 96: Canterbury's stars were the Crusaders' stars as they three-peated – (from left) Justin Marshall, Mehrtens, Caleb Ralph and Greg Somerville.
PAGE 98: Mehrtens was in sublime form.

Mehrtens – who has one of the biggest tickers around – will be able to play the game the only way he knows how. With consummate control."

Another hero on the night, the try-scoring No 8 Ron Cribb, was rewarded with a place in Wayne Smith's first All Blacks squad. Jeff Wilson, Glen Osborne, Darryl Gibson, Carlos Spencer, Rhys Duggan, Dylan Mika, Andrew Blowers, Robin Brooke, Ian Jones, Royce Willis, Greg Feek and Bruce Reihana had all been to the World Cup in 1999 but were all missing from Smith's 26-man squad. As well as Cribb, other newcomers to this new reign included Crusaders players Leon MacDonald, Mark Robinson, Scott Robertson and Greg Somerville, North Harbour's Troy Flavell, Wellington's Pita Alatini and Auckland's Doug Howlett. Todd Blackadder, fresh from lifting the Super 12 trophy for the third time, would be the skipper.

When Smith named his team for the international season opener against Tonga at North Harbour the biggest shock came at No 10 where he opted for Tony Brown ahead of Mehrtens. Any argument that Brown was a better first five-eighth than Mehrtens was destroyed at the 1999 World Cup when Brown replaced an injured Mehrtens for the second spell of the quarterfinal against Scotland. The conclusion of the starting XV for the Tongan test was a suspicion that Smith and his assistant Tony Gilbert did not want to risk one of the All Blacks' key players against the physical and robust tackling expected from the Tongans. But Smith declined to be drawn on the selection saying only: "I'm not making any judgment on who's No 1 or No 2 at this stage. Let them prove

ABOVE: Mehrtens' All Blacks coach was now Wayne Smith.
PAGRE 102: Mehrtens' goal-kicking was key to the Crusaders' phenomenal Super 12 successes.
PAGE 105: Mehrtens has scored more points for New Zealand than any other All Black.
PAGES 106 and 107: Mehrtens bulked up so he could be more combative in internationals.

that on the field. We want to show our confidence in (all of the players) and we want to make everyone feel sure we think they're up to it. And we also want competition for spots and for others to be putting heat on others. So we have placed some new players among some old ones."

The All Blacks scored 15 tries in the 102-0 drubbing. Brown played very well in collecting his 32 points but was replaced by Mehrtens for the test against Scotland at Carisbrook the following weekend. Indeed, Brown wouldn't get another run-on start for the All Blacks in any of the rest of the domestic tests over the next three months.

Despite kicking seven conversions at Carisbrook and a further three at Eden Park in respective 69-20 and 48-14 wins against the Scots, there were some – be it Australians – still prepared to criticise Mehrtens on the eve of the Tri-nations. Queensland Reds coach John Connolly labeled Mehrtens a liability for the All Blacks and said Australia saw the 41-test first five as the weak point in the All Blacks defence. "I know the Australians have an advantage there," Connolly said. "They try to capitalise there because Mehrtens is small and tends to shy away in the tackle. He's quite small whereas Tony Brown is a very strong player and keeps running it to the line."

Mehrtens, unconcerned about Connolly's rant, delivered his own war-cry ahead of the Tri-nations opener at Stadium Australia against the world champion Wallabies. "I think we need to get back to the strengths of New Zealand rugby which is traditionally to get in and smash and intimidate a little bit and I guess do the simple things well," Mehrtens told the *Sunday Star Times*. "That's sort of the opposite to the way they play which means it can be effective if you do it well. We just see them as a good team with a lot of good and skilful players and a team we want to get in and thump. Look at a guy like Troy Flavell, who people have been into the last two or three years about discipline, but look how he's directed it this

year. He's gone through the same processes as I guess Norm Maxwell did a couple of years ago. He's just channelling that energy and raw power. He's just devastating. Most of the guys in this team have had respect for the Aussies for years. We've all grown up playing under-19s and Colts against Australia and they've always been tough sides to beat. We don't see them as suddenly a new kid on the block. We just see them as Australia. They're generally pretty good and you've got to fight hard to win against them."

You've got to fight hard to win against them… prophetic words indeed. The test, played out in front of a world record 109,878, would go down in history as 'The Game Played in Heaven'. The final pass from Taine Rendell to Jonah Lomu in the twilight minutes of the test to deliver the All Blacks a 39-35 win was special enough. But it had nothing on what had preceded it.

In the first minute a clearing kick from Mehrtens was partially charged down by Jason Little. The ball fell to Chris Latham who tried to unload to Joe Roff but Tana Umaga intercepted it and sprinted 45m for the try. Two minutes later it was 14-0 when Ron Cribb unloaded a swift pass to Jonah Lomu on the All Black 22 and the big wing charged 50m down the left flank before unloading to Pita Alatini for the try. By the fifth minute Christian Cullen had scored a try after good work from Alama Ieremia and Alatini. New Zealand led Australia 0. In the eighth minute Mehrtens landed a penalty and a minute later Stirling Mortlock had crashed over for the Wallabies. In the 20th minute Mortlock took a pass from Jim Williams and scored in the corner and six minutes later Chris Latham burst through some weak New Zealand defence to score handy to the posts. Mortlock converted and it was now 24-19. By the 31st minute the game was all tied up after Roff crashed over from close range in the corner.

The Wallabies hit the front six minutes into the second half when Mortlock slotted home a penalty to give the Wallabies a three point advantage. But when Mehrtens converted a Justin Marshall try two minutes

later it was the All Blacks back on top at 31-27. A Mehrtens penalty extended the lead by a further three points before a 62nd minute penalty from Mortlock and a George Gregan inspired Jeremy Paul try gave Australia a 35-34 lead with five minutes on the clock. Then it was time for Randell and Lomu to combine and the All Blacks were triumphant. "I was realistic, even when it got to 24-0," Wayne Smith said. "Against a poor team you often go on to give them a hiding. But Australia are not a poor team – they've got so much resolve and character. We knew they could come back at us and I'm proud of our guys because often when the momentum swings like that you can't halt it. But these guys did and it was a proud moment at the end."

The All Blacks' game against the Springboks seven days later was never going to live up to what occurred in Sydney. But this was a New Zealand/South Africa test match and the build-up certainly didn't disappoint. The 'Boks centre Robbie Fleck and captain Andre Vos said they would target Mehrtens at Jade Stadium. "He has guys inside and outside him who are working hard and can make the tackles if he has too, but he has been exposed at times," Vos said of Mehrtens. "Obviously it is an area we have looked at." Fleck was a little more direct saying: "That is good news (that Mehrtens is playing), it's very good news. I enjoy playing against Alama Ieremia, but defensively, if he was playing, they would be a whole lot stronger. I think it's good news for us because in the channel between Mehrtens and Pita Alatini there's no big hitter."

Wayne Smith laughed off the South African jibes. "We believe (Mehrtens) will make the tackles just like everyone else and we haven't compensated for him. He will have the black jersey on and he's just got to front like he normally does." And like John Connolly before them the South African test stars were embarrassed after the game which was won by the All Blacks 25-12. The 'Boks didn't even score a try while Christian Cullen crossed twice while Mehrtens added

three penalties and a dropped goal before making way late for Tony Brown who added a penalty of his own.

While the All Blacks were 2 and 0 in the Tri-nations, things were far from perfect. The backline wasn't as penetrative as it should have been and the forwards, especially at set-piece – were struggling. And Mehrtens, unhappy with his defensive effort in Sydney, was beating up on himself in the lead-up to the Bledisloe Cup decider at Westpac Trust Stadium in Wellington. "Teams have always had a crack at me but that's probably where a lot of teams attack – first five – because if there's going to be a vulnerable place, that's it," Mehrtens told the *Dominion*. "It's something I've been trying to work on because you don't want to be a weak link on defence or feel like you're not pulling your weight. I was really disappointed with my game against Australia (in Sydney) because I didn't defend very well. It's something I have to work hard on because tackling is not a natural strength, so if my technique is a little bit off they're going to go through me."

Despite his self-confession about his performance in Sydney, Mehrtens had adapted well to the new style of game that had shown itself in 2000. While the World Cup had been a defensive affair, teams were playing with more focus on ball-in-hand attack than the old kick-for-position-and-then-attack routine. "I'm more of a reactive strategist than the tactician five-eighths these days," he said. "You have got to make quick decisions on what you see. You are less in a position now than say, 10 years ago, to be able to sit back and think we will go to here and here and here, because the way the tackle laws are contested now you cannot rely on holding on to the ball for a certain number of phases. I think I am probably being a bit more of a threat at the moment. I know I haven't run a hell of a lot, but I am being a bit more of a threat than I have been in the past couple of years anyway, so that is better."

Another thing on Mehrtens mind before the Bledisloe test was the knowledge that he was poised on the brink of record-breaking greatness. Although he did his best to convince the scribes he wasn't thinking about overtaking Grant Fox as the All Blacks' record points scorer. "The record doesn't enter my head... I'm aware of it, probably more than I let on, because you take a pride in your performance. But I think things like that are something you'll look back on when you stop playing rugby and just take a certain amount of satisfaction in. But what's important to me this weekend is winning the match. That's being completely honest – I would feel I was letting the team or the country down if I was thinking about something personal." Before the test Mehrtens was five points short of Fox's record of 645.

Mehrtens would get the record in the test but it was the Wallabies' inspirational skipper John Eales who stole the headlines with a last second penalty which sealed a 24-23 win.

Mehrtens, who potted two conversions and three penalties, was gutted on what should have been a magical day for him. Mehrtens, already the fastest player to post 600 points in international rugby, broke the All Blacks point-scoring record in 44 tests – two less than Fox. "I'm feeling pretty shattered," he said. "It reduces (the record) to nothing. Milestones are irrelevant when you don't win the game. That's all we came here for. That's all I came here for. Obviously a loss like this hurts. We have to stick tight. The boys have to look after each other. We competed well for the full 80 minutes and to concede 12 points at the start against a team as clinical as Australia and then bag them back was a pretty good achievement. We'd be letting ourselves and our country down if we didn't get over it and get on with the next game. We have to want to improve as much as we can and be up as much as we can for the Ellis Park game."

While Mehrtens wasn't mentioning the record the man who he overtook was talking. "Technically, Andrew is very good," Fox said. "Anyone with his points production is a pivotal force in any game. He has so much influence that when he plays well the All Blacks win and when he is not so good the All Blacks have struggled or lost. He has altered his style to the changing game and I have huge admiration for that."

With a day for the test loss and his record to set in, Mehrtens was ready to talk about his place in history – and he was sure to let everyone know that he thought Fox was still No 1. "Foxy was an icon of New Zealand rugby. He set the benchmark and the standards. I don't know about guys in the past but I think he's been the most accurate and the most consistent of anyone." And Mehrtens played down the importance of the record. "I always despise people who worry just about their own things. But for me alone? We live and die as a team – me as a goal kicker, if a lineout throw doesn't hit the mark, or someone knocks on, we concentrate on the next job."

The next job was the 'Boks at Ellis Park. And Robbie Fleck, who earmarked Mehrtens as a target in Christchurch, was at it again. And this time he had the last laugh – one of his two tries coming after he broke through an attempted tackle from Mehrtens. Incredibly the All Blacks conceded six tries in the game losing 46-40 – the most tries and points conceded by any All Blacks team. Mehrtens' last penalty (his third) and a dropped goal gave New Zealand leads at 37-36 and 40-39 but Werner Swanepoel's second try in the 66th minute, converted by Braam van Straaten, proved the match winner. "(The records) just don't sit with our heritage, our standards or what we're used to. It's disappointing," Wayne Smith said. The All Blacks had lost their Tri-nations crown and the Bledisloe Cup was still safe and secure at the Australian Rugby Union's HQ in Sydney.

There was more disappointment to come for Mehrtens and his Cantabrian All Blacks. Once back in NPC action they steam-rolled the round-robin of the NPC only to lose at home to Wellington in the final. They did win back the Ranfurly Shield – with a 26-18 win against Waikato – but the one-bridge-too-far

ending to the NPC meant the Crusaders' success in May seemed a long time ago as Wayne Smith prepared to name his All Blacks team for the end of year tour to France and Italy. Wellington's success elevated midfield back Jason O'Halloran into the touring side while Greg Feek (Canterbury) and Gordon Slater (Taranaki), Waikato winger-fullback Bruce Reihana, Canterbury second five-eighth Daryl Gibson, Auckland first five-eighth Carlos Spencer and Wellington number eight Filo Tiatia were all restored to the All Blacks.

Spencer's return was deserved. He was back to his best as Auckland finished in second place in the round robin and there was no doubt that – at this stage of the year anyway – he had moved ahead of Tony Brown.

But there was no stopping Mehrtens who, in the opening test on tour, helped the All Blacks to a 39-26 win against the French in Paris. Mehrtens, who kicked 29 points in the victory, had Wayne Smith oozing superlatives. "He's always been a great kicker," Smith said of his first five, "and he's always been a genius, but now I think he can be even better. He's really becoming our nerve centre – everyone trusts him to run the game. He's worked hard on the physical aspects of his game – taking the ball forward and his defence. I think it's created a much better player. He's a much more complete player. He's putting his body on the line."

Seven days later the smile was gone from Smith's face. His team were beaten at Marseilles 42-33. The All Blacks led early in the second half when Mehrtens kicked two of his four penalties on the night, but the team folded again under pressure against the French as they had done a year earlier at Twickenham. Smith, feeling the heat after three test loses, asked for patience from the unforgiving Kiwi public. "I'd hate (the All Blacks) to be labelled as poor test players. They put a lot of heart into today. They've got big careers in front of them. They need a bit of time in the jersey, and need these experiences. It's not about me – it's about the All Blacks. You can hang me. You can do what you like.

"I was quite chuffed that I found myself at the bottom of a ruck and got done over by the Linwood forwards. They've always had a reputation since the likes of Tane Norton of being pretty hard-nosed. I got a couple of welts on my back which was good. It doesn't hurt for long. You turn up in the showers reasonably proud to show your back to everyone, if not your front."

All I want is for the All Blacks to do well. I want to finish my two years and do what I've started. If we get our throats cut, that's the way it is. But if you were in Australian shoes, or French shoes, or South African shoes, would you be beating yourself up for only squaring the series with the All Blacks?"

Smith made four changes for the tour's final game, against Italy in Genoa. And one of them was at first five where Mehrtens was replaced by Carlos Spencer. There were rumors at the time that Mehrtens was culled because he didn't follow the strict instructions coming from the coach's box at the Stade Velodrome. But Smith put the selection down to rotation. "It's an opportunity for Carlos, really," the coach said. "Andrew Mehrtens has had a great season and that continued on last Saturday. My feeling is that he's been the outstanding first five in the world and he can be better too as he starts to run more. And we've got him a bit flatter and he's attacked the defensive lines."

Before the Italian test – which would be won 56-19 – Mehrtens held court with the Italian press and he ended any speculation of a rift between him and Smith when he asked people show faith in the under-pressure coach, and team. "Don't make judgments on what you don't know about is what I'd say. It's very easy to make sweeping statements. Have faith in the guy. They just don't see what's there. They don't know rugby better than he does for starters, so don't try to make comments that suggest they do. He's fully passionate. And you've got to trust that the guys are too. We're not motivated by money. We do care about the All Black jersey. We do care about New Zealand rugby and that's why we're playing it. All the guys could be playing for nothing and they'd still be putting the same effort in. These guys are playing rugby for the right reasons, despite what people may think.

"The public has to believe we think the same things they do. We have the same desire, possibly more, for All Black rugby. We have absolute commitment for

every game and we hurt badly. We hurt worse than people back home when we lose. But we understand people hurt a lot when we lose as well. We understand what we do has a big effect on people back home. They need to know we appreciate that. This team at the moment is benefiting from as much time as we can get together. In that regard it's been beneficial. We're 1-1 with the other three top teams in the world. It's not bad, it's not a disaster. It's not as good as we'd like, but it's a starting point."

Mehrtens also delivered a line the rugby nation had been waiting to hear from someone, anyone! He told the *Sunday Star-Times* the All Blacks were paying a price for being the "nice guys" of world rugby and that it was time the New Zealanders adopted an "if you can't beat 'em, join 'em" attitude. "We do play very fair. I think a lot of the time we give the opposition too much latitude by being so fair. We need that harder edge. The Aussies have been doing it for ages. Auckland did it in their heyday. Just when you're blowing through, holding guys back, little things like that. If you're not getting detected by the ref then you're stupid not to do it. If other teams are doing it to us and getting an advantage, then at the end of the day a result is what you're after. You're still playing within the rules the referee is setting. We've got to be a little more hard-nosed in that regard. If you look back at (French midfield back) Richard Dourthe, I don't think there'd be one ruck he went into without stomping on one of our guys. It was happening in front of referee Jonathan Kaplan all the time. I was right beside him at one point. We had a guy on the ground nowhere near the ball; Dourthe comes flying in just all over the top of him. It's just little things like that."

They were inspiring words but Mehrtens' own career was on hold at the beginning of 2001. He knew even before the All Blacks tour to France and Italy that he would miss the early stages of the Super 12 after aggravating a groin injury. He had been relying on anti-inflammatories as well as a strict warm-up and

stretching regime before and after training and matches. The adductor muscle of his right leg had been the initial problem, caused by kicking, but the whole upper thigh area and joint had been gradually affected. "It's not a chronic problem, it's a use problem." he said. "I just found it really, really hard to accelerate. It took me ages to warm up. During the kicking motion, side-on, it was really painful as well."

Mehrtens was advised by experts to start a regular stretching routine. "What seemed to help was taking anti-inflammatories. You never want to rely on them but every time I go off them I stiffen up again. I'm not making it any worse by training and playing. I've talked to doctors about it and about using anti-inflammatories. They said the fact that they worked so effectively just meant the whole area has got strain on it, just inflammation – not necessarily muscle damage. Maybe a rest of up to six weeks or a couple of months – staying away from the dynamic running to allow it to simmer down – is probably the best thing for it when the season's over."

Mehrtens missed the pre-season and opening two rounds of the Super 12 as the defending champions lost to the Brumbies and Blues. He made the bench for the Chiefs game (won 40-11) but was not used and came on in the 32-26 win against the Reds. He started in the loss against the Hurricanes, was ill and missed the Bulls game and was only picked on the bench for the Stormers game in Cape Town. With that game lost

ABOVE: Injuries meant Mehrtens played a support role for his team.
OPPOSITE: Mehrtens' could always see the funny side of life – even with a strapped leg...
PAGE 112: Mehrtens was as passionate as anyone about the All Blacks haka.

49-28, Mehrtens was restored to No 10 jersey for the loss against the Cats in Nelson and was then dropped from the squad. *Dropped*. And the rumors of a rift between Mehrtens and Deans were at a fever pitch. "Selection," Deans said, "is based on what's good for the team in any given circumstance and that can change from week to week. We can't look at it in isolation – we look at it within the context of the team and continuity is very important in a team game and that's what we've gone for." Mehrtens – Canterbury's favourite son was told to play club rugby. "Once we made the decision who to start we felt it best that Mehrts, rather than sitting on the bench, get a full 80 minutes of rugby and, as a consequence, he's playing club rugby," Deans said. "It's very evident that Mehrts came into the season behind the eight-ball after his groin injury and its taken time. He's only had two starts and one run-on, that's a contributing factor to his form."

All Black coaches Wayne Smith and Tony Gilbert watched from the bank at Linwood's Linfield Park, with Robbie Deans and Steve Hansen watching from the club lounge. Mehrtens helped High School Old Boys to a 28-17 win. "It's like this," he explained as he signed autographs after the game, "I've never wanted to give interviews unless I have something to talk about. Right now I really don't think the story is about me, it's about the guys who are playing for the Crusaders."

At one stage in the game he dived into a ruck to try to prove he wasn't afraid of the rough stuff. Linwood hooker Craig Randall spotted the All Blacks first five and gave him a rucking welcome back to club rugby. "But I enjoyed it," Mehrtens said. "I was quite chuffed that I found myself at the bottom of a ruck and got done over by the Linwood forwards. They've always had a reputation since the likes of Tane Norton of being pretty hard-nosed. I got a couple of welts on my back which was good. It doesn't hurt for long. You turn up in the showers reasonably proud to show your back to everyone, if not your front." Not everyone agreed with the treatment dished out to Mehrtens. Randall was

called out by the referee and sin-binned for excessive rucking. Mehrtens' reaction was unscripted. Instead of looking for sympathy he begged the referee to call the hooker back onto the field. "I was stunned when the poor joker got sin-binned," he said. "I asked the referee not to do it. I didn't want him to be sin-binned. Rucking is bloody important. If you end up on the wrong side of the ruck you deserve to wear a few sprigs. As long as it's not stomping to the head then it's all right."

Mehrtens said he enjoyed getting back and playing at club grounds he hadn't played on for eight or nine years. "In fact I loved it. It dragged me up in a way and it seems about 80 percent of guys playing club rugby now are 18 or 19. They have a huge amount of energy, are great fellas, and made me feel a bit younger. I don't smoke but one thing I enjoyed, while it's probably not politically correct, is that you walk off the ground at Old Boys, walk across the road to the clubrooms and there are a couple of guys on the veranda having a cigarette and drinking a couple of beers. The whole environment seemed really relaxed. Guys worked hard on the field but it was a blast from the past off it. It's a hell of a shame All Blacks can't play club rugby more often."

Smith was backing Mehrtens to come good in time for the internationals. "I believe Andrew Mehrtens ranks with Grant Fox as our greatest first fives. So it's a shame to see the situation he's in. But only he can fix things. It's going to take a lot of hard work… he's got to commit to that hard work and I'm certain he can turn it around. It's a major concern for me. He hasn't just been a key part of All Black teams, he's been a key part of my Crusader teams. You can go as far to say that if we didn't have him in 1998 and 1999 I don't think we would have won the Super 12. That's not degrading anyone else and I think even the players would say that themselves."

"I back the Super 12 coaches… they are their teams. Robbie Deans has made a choice of going for someone with better form (Aaron Mauger). I discussed it with Robbie and, given that situation, I think it's great Andrew went back to his club to get 80 minutes of rugby. Ideally, he now makes the last two Super 12 games, but that's up to him and the Crusaders."

Deans left Mehrtens out of the squad for the game against the Waratahs in Sydney. Former All Blacks were being quoted everywhere. Jeff Wilson said Mehrtens was burnt out. Chris Laidlaw said Mehrtens should be playing. Richard Loe said Deans was mad. And the French club Biarritz even linked themselves to 'the want-away star'. Mehrtens finally broke his silence in the week leading up to the Crusaders' last game of the season against the Highlanders. He addressed his supposed issue with Deans and the rumours that had been circulating about his alleged drinking.

"I've heard I'm having a bitter feud (with Deans) but that's not the case. I know I'm not giving my best to the team. I expected no special treatment. We pride ourselves here that we're all equal. I haven't been hard done by. That's why I haven't said anything up to now. I didn't see it as an issue. But I'm keen as hell to play rugby. I've had a reasonably difficult injury, in there wasn't one simple solution for it and it's created a lot of its own problems. I haven't been able to train fully for four months. I just hung out in Queenstown and didn't do a lot (of training). I had a quiet summer and I certainly wasn't on the juice (alcohol). The guys have been reasonably careful. Over the last four or five years everyone has learnt how to look after themselves a wee bit better in terms of training. You can't compromise your teammates by hitting the booze all the time."

Deans picked Mehrtens for the game in Dunedin. The Crusaders' season had been a disaster. Only four wins going into the last weekend of the round-robin meant that playoff rugby was literally a mile away. As it was the Southern derby would be lost as well and the champions had finished well off the pace in 10th place. Mehrtens' game at Carisbrook was average. He had a kick charged down within 15 seconds of the kickoff which led to a Highlanders try. But he composed himself and played solidly as he grabbed three penalties. Attention now quickly turned to the naming of the All Blacks.

IT was like 1998 all over again. All the self-doubt, the second guessing, the losses (although not as many)… the rugby nation was in turmoil. And as one All Blacks first five was on his way out (read: Wayne Smith) another (read: Andrew Mehrtens) was up for the fight of his life.

WHEN Smith named his All Blacks squad the biggest surprise was not that Mehrtens was there (which he was) but that Todd Blackadder wasn't. Smith – the most loyal of coaches – had axed his former Crusaders captain and given the leadership to Otago's Anton Oliver. Ahead of the team were tests against Samoa, Argentina and France before a Tri-nations campaign and end-of-year tour to Ireland, Scotland and Argentina.

Smith knew he needed Mehrtens at his best and quickly. "I've spent some time with Andrew," Smith said before the All Blacks assembled. "I've been with the Crusaders players… they are training once a day together, as are all the squad members in their regions. They have to be up to speed with moves and calls before we go into camp so we can maximize our time there. Mehrts has worked hard and he needed to. He has set his targets high as we have as coaches. But I think we have seen a significant lift in his training and his play over the last few weeks. He just has to keep going at it."

Smith opted to play the Otago inside backs – Byron Kelleher and Tony Brown – against the Samoans at North Harbour with Mehrtens and Justin Marshall on the bench. And after the All Blacks' first up 50-6 victory, the roles were reversed for the one-off test against Argentina at Jade Stadium. Mehrtens made a slick return to test action banging over a perfect four-from-four kicks and throwing some key cutout passes to put the speedsters into the gaps in a 67-19 win. But his comeback test was cut-short when he left the field with a deep-seated bruise to a quadricep.

The injury meant he was in a race against time to be fit to play against the French at Westpac Trust Stadium in Wellington. He was initially left out of the 15 and bracketed with Mark Ranby on the bench. He would be cleared to play the test on the Saturday but was not used as Brown was in commanding form during the 37-12 win. Brown, who'd scored three tries against Samoa two weeks earlier, slotted four conversions and three penalties against the French. "Myself and Mehrts get on very well," Brown told reporters after the test. "He supports me and I support him. As long as the team does well, we're both happy."

How happy Mehrtens was when the test side to play against the 'Boks at Newlands in Cape Town was named is debatable. Brown was in the starting XV ahead of Mehrtens. And there was no injury in play here – this was all about form. "We know they (South Africa) are going to try and outmuscle us," Smith said. "We know they're going to attack down the first five-eighth channel, so we decided to go again with Tony. He played really well against Samoa and France and when he came on against Argentina, so he's a player in form, and he's tough down that channel."

Anton Oliver said Brown had played well enough to be retained. "It's good news for Tony, because now that Andrew's fit and ready to go, Tony's still been given

ABOVE: On the charge against Samoa, Tony Brown emerged as a real threat to Mehrtens' hold on the All Blacks No 10 jersey.
PAGE 116: Mehrtens, with Byron Kelleher, was battling Tony Brown for the All Blacks No 10 jersey.
PAGES 118 AND 119: Mehrtens was all class as Canterbury dismantled Auckland in a Shield game.
PAGES 120 AND 121: The Crusaders went through the Super 12 unbeaten.
PAGE 123: Two key men in the Canterblacks – Crusaders coach Robbie Deans and his skipper Reuben Thorne.

the spot. And that's good for the rest of the guys in the team. They know now that if they get in and play well, then (the selectors) will show trust in you and pick you again. This is despite the fact Andrew's got such a good record and been such a good All Black."

Brown thrived in the physical battle at Newlands. He collected all of New Zealand's points form penalties as the All Blacks won 12-3. "Tony's clearly answered any critics so far," Smith said. "He plays a certain style, but he's not one-dimensional – he's working on other sides of his game. He's a different player from Andrew. They're both world-class. I think that the difference has been this year that Tony has moved up to be a world-class five-eighth, and it's great to have that sort of competition there. We always look at who we're playing, and we also do reverse analysis. We look at how we think they'll be looking at us, how they think we'll play, where they think our strengths and weaknesses are, and we'll try to adapt accordingly."

Once back in New Zealand, the writing seemed to be on the wall for Mehrtens when Brown was given a weekend off with the Cantabrian – stuck on 49 tests – sent off to play for Old Boys in the Christchurch club final. And while Mehrtens' deeds for his club were being reported on one page of the Sunday papers (he kicked a last minute penalty to help Old Boys to a 23-20 win against Christchurch) Smith was on another page praising Brown. "Tony Brown has proven things to me in every match," Smith told the *Sunday Star Times*. "It's great to have another world class five-eighths operating. We know we have Carlos there and Mehrts… the depth there is really pleasing and Tony has added to that. He has some special skills. You don't attack down his channel and the Springboks found that out. We've also been really happy with his goal kicking. He's on 11 out of 11 with his kicks at the moment, so he's building a good sequence there."

There were no surprises when Brown was named at first five for the Bledisloe Cup test at Dunedin. The Otago stalwart saw the test as a chance to contest the

tactical battle against Stephen Larkham "who's the best first-five in the world, at this stage." Brown said, "It'll be good to match myself against him. He's proved himself the best in the world, in the international arena."

Brown came up short in the contest, as did the All Blacks going down 23-15. Their Tri-nations chances also suffered when Anton Oliver bizarrely turned down a late penalty that if Mehrtens (on the field as a replacement) had kicked would have given the team an important bonus point for losing by less than seven points. The All Blacks trailed 23-15 at the time of the penalty.

Oliver's decision meant the Eden Park test against South Africa in two weeks time was a must-win affair. And he turned to Mehrtens to help get the team the 'W'. And with him into the team came Byron Kelleher while Brown and Justin Marshall were out. "I feel a bit sorry for Justin and Tony Brown," Smith said. "The change, in many ways, was a consequence of bad ball in Dunedin – and hopefully it won't happen again to these two.

"That's not all the fault of those two players. But these two guys (Mehrtens and Kelleher) are looking snappy."

Kelleher would be the star of the 26-15 win. His work around the rucks and quick passes helped ignite the All Blacks into action. Mehrtens too would have been happy with a performance that saw him land two conversions and four penalties. Wrote Simon Winter in the *Sunday News*: "Mehrtens put his injuries behind him, expertly marshalling the All Blacks backs. Mehrtens' long, raking kicks downfield kept the Springboks on the back foot. His cut-out passes across the midfield also provided his backs with extra space."

Wayne Smith too had a word of praise for his first five. "Mehrts was tactically superb. I thought we were brilliant. It's good to see the improvement."

The next game – a Bledisloe Cup and Tri-nations decider – was set for Sydney's Stadium Australia the following weekend. It would prove to be an extraordinarily important test for All Blacks rugby. As the match ticked into the last two minutes, and the All Blacks were handed a royal chance to see off the Wallabies but the lineout wobbles struck again.

A penalty was awarded, deep in the heart of their territory, Mehrtens found touch and, unbelievably, the All Blacks coughed up the ball on their own throw to enable the Wallabies to storm back onto attack. No 8 Toutai Kefu took the ball on the cutback, powering through Ron Cribb's attempted tackle and crossing near the posts to secure a 29-26 win.

Smith was rattled. With the Bledisloe and Tri-nations title lost, he called for calm. "I hope the public understand what these guys put into the match," he said. "To me, as a New Zealander, I'm proud of them. I don't expect a ticker tape parade but I think New Zealanders will appreciate the heart and spirit that was shown." But Smith had made serious blunders through the campaign. Overlooking Mehrtens in the earlier tests, not using Christian Cullen from the start in Sydney, banking on a skipper who hadn't mastered the art of the lineout throw… these were all major problems.

There's no doubt Smith felt the pressure of the loss. Some have said he was in tears in the changing sheds after the test. Seventeen days after the loss his fate was sealed when he faced a New Zealand Rugby Football Union review committee. In his caring, sharing way he felt it was up to others to make the decision on his future rather than he campaign to stay. So HQ's brains trust made their decision – Smith and Tony Gilbert were out and John Mitchell and Robbie Deans were in.

Mehrtens by now was back to his best for Canterbury in the NPC. He showed off his wizardry in the 38-10 Ranfurly Shield dismantling of Auckland and told reporters after the game that he was keen to join the new coaches on the tour to Ireland, Scotland and Argentina. "From an individual point of view if I was picked I would be keen as hell. It's one of those things you make the call when you come to it. Nobody

assumes selection anyway. When I think about it, guys would be within their rights and it would be understandable if some wanted to go to opt out."

Mehrtens had gotten over the misery of Sydney by spending time with his one-year-old son, Sam, and his former partner and manager Jacki Wong. In an interview with *Woman's Day* magazine, Mehrtens revealed his personal life is also back on track after the traumatic split with Wong, which led to regrets and heavy drinking. He has since rebuilt his relationship and the pair have reconciled to the point where they both spend time with Sam. Mehrtens said it was hard to be away from Sam and his mother. "I've learned a lot about how to switch on and off from my rugby. I have to accept that I can't do anything for Sam when I'm at training or away, but when I come back and I'm with him I concentrate on his needs at the time – not dwell on whether it's been a bad session or a bad game." Wong said Mehrtens was much more than a "good times" dad. "I'm very spoilt," she said. "He could be half as good or a third as good and still be a superb father. Sam is a lucky little boy."

Mehrtens could have been feeling lucky when John Mitchell named his first All Blacks squad. After helping Canterbury to the NPC title it was a given that he would be selected. But when Christian Cullen, Jeff Wilson and Taine Randell were all left out of the side, everyone named felt lucky not to have been made an example out of. Mehrtens, while gutted for his long-term teammates, confirmed his place as the best first five in the country by playing full games in the test wins against Ireland (40-29), Scotland (37-6) and Argentina (24-20).

He continued his match-winning form in the 2002 Super 12 outplaying his All Blacks rivals Tony Brown and Carlos Spencer as the Crusaders – after the disappointments of the previous season – went through the season unbeaten, beating the Brumbies in the final at Jade Stadium 31-13. Comments by Wallabies wing Wendell Sailor after Mehrtens had weaved his magic against the Reds in Brisbane were typical of others made during the competition. "Andrew Mehrtens is a freak," Sailor said. "He's just too good. In league, our equivalent is Andrew Johns (the Newcastle, New South Wales, and Australia scrum-half). It's just like everything comes second nature to them. It just looks effortless when he runs around. I was a bit nervous tonight. You don't know what he (Mehrtens) is going to do – put it behind you, in the air, run it, or throw it, and that's a player with a lot of class, and a lot of time on his hands."

And Robbie Deans – with his Crusaders' coach's hat on – paid Mehrtens the ultimate tribute when he said he was now a "complete player". Said Deans: "Mehrts has been defending really well in the last few rounds. It's something he's put a lot of work into, and he's seeing the benefits of it. It's great. He's now the complete player."

There was little surprise when 15 Canterbury players were named in Mitchell and Deans' All Blacks squad. Crusaders skipper Reuben Thorne was confirmed as the new All Blacks captain and midfield backs Daryl Gibson and Mark Robinson were recalled after a two-year absence. In the first test of the year, a 64-10 win against Italy in Hamilton, Mehrtens became a world record holder after a near-perfect night, with eight conversions and a penalty. His 146 test conversions overtook Australian Michael Lynagh's previous world record of 140.

The following weekend the term 'Canterblacks' was born when John Mitchell named 13 Crusaders in the All Blacks' run-on side against Ireland in Dunedin. The standout players in the 15-6 win were Mehrtens and his Crusaders' second-five Aaron Mauger. The 21 year old former NZ Colts skipper was loving his armchair ride outside the master. "It's great playing with Mehrts. He's good fun on the field and he seems to create a lot more space for his outsides than most first fives do. That makes your job easier."

The duo were together again for the second Irish test in Auckland. This time there were 14 Crusaders in the side – Jonah Lomu the only non-Cantabrian in the XV. The 40-8 score line showed some signs of improvement from the team although the word 'skittery' was used in more than one match report the following day.

Mauger was given the start at No 10 for the one-off test against Fiji in Wellington and looked comfortable throughout the 68-18 victory. But Mehrtens was restored to the side for the opening Bledisloe and Tri-nations game at Jade Stadium. And in the build up to the test Mehrtens found himself coming to defence of the All Blacks coaches who had been painted in a dour and unflattering light in Sydney by *Sydney Morning Herald* columnist Spiro Zavos.

He described Mitchell as "grim-faced, laconic, and traditional in his approach to how test rugby should be played." And while the two tests against Ireland in particular had indeed been dour, Mehrtens put the case for his coach saying "we're not robots". He admitted the All Blacks were becoming too pre-planned. When that happened the players looked at the next phase and ignored what chances were on. "We're trying to concentrate on everyone assuming we're going to have a crack at that phase, rather than we're setting to move. Otherwise it becomes predictable who is getting the ball. What you need is everyone reacting as if you don't know what is going (if you are) to adequately threaten the opposition defence."

Before the test Mehrtens talked of the hurt of so many recent loses to the Wallabies. "Losing seven from nine is not something we dwell a lot on. Obviously we don't like it but it doesn't really do anything for this week. When you start talking about statistics like that, how far back do you go? If you go back 40 years, the record is probably something like New Zealand 27 Australia 13 (actually, it was New Zealand 42 Australia 22). The desire to win this game is 100 percent. If we had won seven out of nine, my desire would be no less to win this game. Obviously having lost two last year, the country is pretty much crying out for us to beat

ABOVE: Mehrtens wanted the All Blacks to get a bit more ruthless – like the 'Boks.

PAGE 127: Mehrtens was stunned when Carlos Spencer was named ahead of him for the test against England in 2002.

Australia. Certainly not having had the Bledisloe Cup for the last four or five years, we're sick of hearing about the bulging Australian trophy cabinet. Everyone's like that, we're no different. I hope everyone trusts us that we'll give it our everything."

Do we rate the Wallabies too highly in this country? "A lot of the time, what your guys' (media) perception of other teams is not quite what ours are," Mehrtens said. "Look at Ireland. Nobody seemed to have a lot of respect for Ireland apart from us because we know how tough they are to play. I think you'll find the South African media are more complimentary towards us than they are to their own players. Because you want so much for your own team to win, you tend to be a lot more critical and analytical about it but you take other teams on face value."

Why have Australia been so successful? "They're pretty ruthless. When they get opportunities they tend to take them. Their handling is really good on the outside and their support play is good. It just seems that when things start to meander along for them, they just hit something with urgency and get a lot of go-forward. They've probably had more belief in themselves for the last three or four years. Rather than getting intimidated like they used to. Certainly they've improved a huge amount since they were called the Woeful Wallabies. That's a thing of the past."

By the end of the test the All Blacks had one hand on the Bledisloe Cup. In a try-less encounter Mehrtens (four penalties) had beaten Matthew Burke (two penalties). "This result has made (the Bledisloe) exciting," Mehrtens said. "The Bledisloe Cup is just one win away now. We've beaten the world cup holders and we have every reason to celebrate. It was a fantastic team win. We'd like to think we scored a bloody good win. I'm just delighted." Mehrtens was one of the heroes of the All Blacks' gutsy effort. He'd revelled in the high pressure and controlled the game with some superb tactical kicking.

A week later – after a 41-20 win against the Springboks in Wellington – Mehrtens was even more confident of Bledisloe Cup success in Sydney. "We're achieving a higher standard of consistency," he said after landing two conversions, three penalties and a dropped goal against the 'Boks. "The feeling is we are not capable of the huge inconsistencies we were capable of in the last four or five years. There's a saying that even when you hold the Ranfurly Shield, you go out to attack to win it back again. I think most rugby is like that these days. It's not really an option to shut down a game. We want to have a go. We don't want to come off (against the Wallabies) and feel like we haven't really given it a crack."

It could be argued that is exactly what happened. The All Blacks were off the pace from the get-go at Telstra Stadium – Mehrtens missing his first two kicks at goal. And the killer instinct was with the Australians and not the New Zealanders in the do-or-die game won by the home side 16-14. "We were probably a little too fair out there at times," Mehrtens said. "Maybe we needed to push the boundaries in the same way that they were. We were backing our defence. We've never really been a team that has got in and tried to cheat. I still don't know what happened at the end but we're not going to have a witch hunt or anything." What happened was that Matthew Burke had landed a last second penalty to steal the win from the All Blacks – John Mitchell's first loss as coach.

While the Bledisloe Cup was Australia's for another year, a win against the 'Boks in Durban would secure the Tri-nations championship. The test would be

best remembered for the attack on referee David McHugh. The Irishman was crash-tackled from behind by a spectator about a minute into the second half of the All Blacks' 30-23 win. He was forced from the field with a dislocated shoulder and fainted with pain under the Kings Park grandstand. Back on the field the All Blacks scored four tries and secured the points to land the Tri-nations trophy.

After the win, Mehrtens was charged with serious misconduct for criticising South African rugby referee Andre Watson after the Sydney Bledisloe Cup test. Mehrtens had said Watson should be "ashamed" of his performance. "I'm not sure if Australia deserved to win. We probably lost the game more so, but we were helped to lose it obviously," he said, referring to Watson. "He should be more ashamed than some of us should be."

South Africa Rugby managing director Rian Oberholzer reacted by writing to the NZRU asking it to discipline Mehrtens. "We take a dim view of the comments made by the All Blacks player and we are expecting New Zealand to do the same," Oberholzer said. "We cannot take any action ourselves. We have written to the NZRU to ask them to look into the matter." The NZRU's Steve Tew said: "The referees don't criticise players or coaches and they do their best. There is a process by which they are evaluated and selected and that's where their performance should be judged." He then fined Mehrtens $2000.

Despite being offside with HQ – or perhaps because of it – the great Buck Shelford came out in support of Mehrtens as All Blacks captain for the end of year tour to England, France and Wales. With former skipper Anton Oliver and current captain Reuben Thorne both injured John Mitchell was on the look out for a new captain. "Until Thorne and Oliver return, they'll need to appoint someone who can demand a place in the team and I reckon the man for the job could be Mehrts. He has a wealth of experience, and he's one of the few blokes who you know will be there every week. He's been making a lot of the calls and running play for years."

When Mitchell named the team the skipper was Taine Randell. And he was leading a 26-man squad that included 12 uncapped players as many of the front-line players were given the summer off to ready themselves for the 2003 World Cup. The new caps included five from Auckland's dominant NPC team Steve Devine, Daniel Braid, Keven Mealamu, Brad Mika, and Ali Williams, Waikato's Regan King, Keith Lowen, and Keith Robinson, Otago halfback Danny Lee, Taranaki hooker Andrew Hore, North Harbour prop Tony Woodcock and Wellington loose forward Rodney So'oialo. And Carlos Spencer was back and once again breathing down Mehrtens' neck.

Mehrtens believed he needed to do more on attack after he meandered through too many games this year. "There were times when I ran more and was an attacking presence, but there were other times when I felt I wasn't doing anything except calling the moves and passing the ball – being a distributor. I feel like a lot of the time I meandered through the games. It's tough at first five because you want to give the other backs a chance and we know how good they can be. But you also have the responsibility to commit defences more than I have."

In a sense the pressure was off on this tour. With so many first-choice All Blacks being rested expectations for the tests at Twickeham, Stade de France and the Millennium Stadium were low. But Mehrtens was nevertheless confident about the first-up assignment in London. "The All Blacks have never lacked for motivation against England. Talk to any All Black that's lost to them and they say it's a painful experience. They are horrible to lose to and we found them even painful to draw with in 1997. So there's no lacking in motivation."

Mitchell stunned everyone when he named Carlos Spencer at first five ahead of Mehrtens – especially since Mehrtens had been required to front press-conferences leading up to the test. "I've naturally been excited by Carlos' form in the NPC this year," Mitchell explained. "It's not so much the unpredictableness or flair, I think flair's overrated. I think he's a very mature player, who's contributed extremely well to Auckland's success this season. He's probably run more creative lines as a five-eighths this year and put other players into space."

Robbie Deans was wheeled out to support the head coach's decision. "We're reinforcing performance, if you like," Deans said. "Carlos has come out of the NPC where he's played very well. He's brought a degree of maturity to his game that's been assisted by the performance of people around him, where he hasn't been forced to try and do the miraculous. We're lucky we've got two great five-eighths, and they'll both get starts. But Carlos has come out of the NPC final, he's on fire, so we'll just keep him going." Deans said Mehrtens took his non-selection well. "Mehrts is great ... he's a great servant of New Zealand rugby. He's had highs and he's had lows. He doesn't see it as not being involved."

Spencer struggled at Twickenham. He looked sluggish and was caught with the ball a number of times. When Mehrtens replaced him in the second half the All Blacks played with a better tempo. It was too little too late though – England had won 31-28.

With Spencer battling a shoulder injury Mehrtens was given the start against the French a week later. And Mehrtens was fired up for action. That was clear when he was asked about comments made by England coach Clive Woodward about perceived All Black obstruction at Twickers. "Woodward had a crack at me, saying I should do my talking on the field – that's rich coming from him," he told the *Guardian*.

"England get a decent win about every four years at Twickenham, and they act like this every time. Although having said that, I wouldn't call their last couple of wins over South Africa and Australia 'decent'. We're (Southern Hemisphere teams) at the end of our seasons, and two years ago they needed a video

referee to award the winning try over a 13-man Aussie team. Great win that one. I can't believe that guy sometimes."

Mehrtens was on a roll. His next target was *The Times* rugby writer Stephen Jones who repeated his theory that the Southern Hemisphere's Super 12 competition was not of a high standard. "After an extraordinary day of international rugby, the balance of power of the global game has tilted irresistibly toward the north," Jones wrote. "What was striking about all three games is the fact that the home teams battered their opponents in the forward play. This is a stunning reversal of history and further evidence, of the softening effect on forward play below the equator caused by the relative powder- puff nature of the Super 12 competition."

Mehrtens laughed off the comments. "They can say what they like, how many English players have excelled in the Super 12? How many have been bothered to come out and play it? Whereas we've got old, retired New Zealanders and up-and-coming New Zealanders who go and excel in the premiership there (England). Not that I'm trying to run down their competition or anything but they've always been the ones who have abused the Super 12."

The balance of power titled back towards the Southern Hemisphere when the All Blacks took on France. The under-strength All Blacks held on for a 20-20 draw. Said Mitchell: "considering the youthfulness of some of these players on tour, it's incredible. And I suppose, in some ways, we might have achieved a moral victory as a team today."

ABOVE: Mehrtens' kicking was key on the end-of-year tour in 2002.
LEFT: Mehrtens went high against England – before going low when taking on the media after the loss.
PAGES 132 AND 133: The one place Mehrtens wanted to be in 2003 – amongst the Men in Black.

Mehrtens would win his 66th test cap against Wales in the tour's final game. It made him the third-most-capped All Black of all time. Only Sean Fitzpatrick (90) and Ian Jones (79) had played more tests. And fittingly, with five new caps on the pitch, he helped lead the All Blacks to an impressive 43-17 win by landing four conversions and five penalties.

HOPE floats eternal. When you haven't won the World Cup since 1987 it has too. Because there is no immediate record of success at World Cups all you can do is hope the men charged with winning it, are on the right course. And so it seemed with John Mitchell and Robbie Deans in 2003.

AN all-New Zealand Super 12 final – won by the Blues against the Crusaders – meant that many of the players that were meant to be were in form. The fact that the Hurricanes had made the semi finals gave further hope that things were progressing well. The emergence of Aaron Mauger and Dan Carter at the Crusaders meant that there was some new blood to go with the experience of Andrew Mehrtens and Carlos Spencer.

But this has been no ordinary year for Mehrtens. Rumors of a rift between him and Deans had surfaced again. And they'd been growing in intensity since the opening round of the Super 12 when Deans had benched the All Blacks incumbent and selected Carter instead. In the second round he started against the Reds before going off with a knee injury. He wouldn't be sighted in the comp again until the ninth round. After playing against the Bulls and Stormers, he missed the last round robin game against the Brumbies with a hand injury. Despite bring fit for the semifinal against the Hurricanes, Deans opted to start Aaron Mauger at first five. And it was the same for the final. It was hardly the endorsement Mehrtens and his supporters were looking for in a World Cup year.

Mehrtens' fate was sealed when he was left out of the squad named for the home tests against England, Wales and France. John Mitchell and Robbie Deans favoured inside backs were Carlos Spencer, Dan Carter and Aaron Mauger. Also missing from the All Blacks were Taine Randell and Christian Cullen who, along with Mehrtens, where named in the wider All Blacks group. "We haven't seen enough evidence of Andrew in this competition," Mitchell said of Mehrtens' Super 12. "There are a couple of areas in his game that we would like him to improve on looking to the end of the year. The rest of the season is really up to Andrew. We know a lot about his past form and what he can offer but players at the moment that have been ranked ahead of him are clearly better, we believe, at taking the ball to the attacking line and defending."

Grant Fox – the All Blacks legend – was stunned with Mehrtens' omission. "Mehrtens is a great player and I don't use that term lightly. I rarely use it, but this guy is a great player. He has a proven track record and offers quite a different style of game to Carlos." Mitchell though continued to praise Spencer over the next week. "Carlos is an all round player now," said Mitchell. "His decision-making has got better and it's a vote of confidence to him that he's the No 1 five-eighth in our selection. He has really made strides, particularly with his kicking game. We rewarded him last year at Twickenham. Unfortunately, he got an injury and he has rehabilitated that rather than getting surgery. You have to admire the guy's tenacity and mental strength to do that and come back stronger."

After a 15-13 loss to England and wins against Wales (55-3) and France (31-23) there were calls for Mehrtens to be reinstated for the Tri-nations. "Can the All Blacks do without Andrew Mehrtens?" asked the *Dominion's* columnist, former All Blacks Chris Laidlaw. "On the face of it, no. Mehrtens has been the victim of a cruelly timed injury, something that has opened the door wide to other five-eighths this year. Carlos Spencer and Daniel Carter have charged through. There

"I just can't wait and am itching to step out there.
The thrill will be even better this time round. Even a little bit more so,
because when I first got in the All Blacks it happened so quickly.
Everything was new whereas having had the time off last year
I knew what it meant to me. You can't cherish it until you've got it
and I really cherish it a lot more this time."

seems to be a working assumption that, with Spencer as first choice, then Carter and if necessary Aaron Mauger as the third option, the first five base is adequately covered. But is it? Mauger should have become the natural successor to Mehrtens but he too has been on and off this year, largely due to injury. Carter has become a cover player for first and second five-eighths but is unproven against the toughest of competition. That leaves Spencer as the only specialist and that makes many of us nervous.

"Spencer showed he can occasionally beat even the best defence in the business – against the English – but he also showed, again against England and earlier in the season against the Highlanders, that he can be boxed into corners and made indecisive. The English and the Wallabies will work on ways of shutting down the Spencer one-man act and you can be fairly sure that nothing much will be left to chance. They would prefer Spencer as an opponent to a fully functional Mehrtens because – now the All Black forwards can more or less guarantee parity of possession – Mehrtens is much more capable of tactically destroying another team. And there is the issue of goal kicking. Neither Spencer nor Carter provides the degree of confidence Mehrtens does."

Mitchell and Deans stuck to their guns and ignored Mehrtens when they named their squad for the Tri-nations. And they could argue they were justified in doing that as the All Blacks ran riot in the competition winning both the Tri-nations Trophy and Bledisloe Cups with some devastatingly good rugby including record wins against the 'Boks (52-16) and Wallabies (50-21).

But with a World Cup squad of 30 to be named it would seem foolhardy not to pick Mehrtens – even if only for the experience he could bring coming off the bench. Indeed, while the country debated Mitchell's selections a *Sunday Star-Times* competition to select the greatest All Black team ever – Sir Wilson Whineray, Fred Allen and Alex Wyllie – selected Mehrtens at first

five. They swayed towards 66-test veteran Mehrtens, whose 14.1-points-per-test average just nudges Grant Fox's 14, as he was the superior attacker. Fox agreed with the judges. "Absolutely. He's been a great servant to All Black rugby. He's a great and I don't use the word 'great' very often," Fox said. "And I don't want to sound like I'm speaking of him in past tense because I think there's life in the old bugger yet."

Former All Black first five Earl Kirton said there should be room for the mercurial Cantabrian in Mitchell's World Cup squad. "I'd have him in the squad, of course I would," he said. "But the other guy (Carlos Spencer) has been playing damn well to be fair. I think they will take him; they're just geeing him up, giving him bit of a nudge." Spencer was not nominated for best No 10 but Fox agreed there was room for both first fives in the World Cup squad. "From a personal point of view I like the idea of contrast and with Andrew and Carlos you have a nice contrast. It allows you to have flexibility in your game plan."

Mehrtens, Taine Randell, Christian Cullen and Anton Oliver all missed selection and the country was in an outrage. Despite the successes against Australia and South Africa there was a general feeling that Mitchell's squad lacked experience. And that perception was right. Tana Umaga was injured in the first game of the tournament and by the time of the semifinal against Australia Carlos Spencer had the goal kicking responsibilities taken off him and they were handed to the make-shift centre Leon MacDonald. In the semi Spencer – who would be later dubbed Hope'Los – threw an intercepted pass and

ABOVE: Robbie Deans and Mehrtens enjoyed many great moments at the Crusaders but it didn't mean Deans would pick him for the 2003 World Cup.

the All Blacks crashed out of the tournament. And in an ironic twist, Mitchell, at his last press conference as coach, admitted his team "lacked experienced". Doh!

MOST mere mortals would have packed up and headed off-shore. But not Andrew Mehrtens. Not yet. In the aftermath of the World Cup debacle he had the chance to head to the Sharks in South Africa or his pick of European teams. But Mehrtens wasn't even tempted. He was desperate to wear the black jersey again.

TOWARDS the end of 2003 – a year where he was completely shut out of the All Blacks – Mehrtens re-signed with the NZRU for another year. "I've signed for another year, with a view to seeing how it pans out next year," the now 30-year-old said. "I would love to stick around and have no great desire to go overseas, especially while I'm enjoying my rugby here. You respect the guys that are leaving and moving on to different challenges, but I've still got things I want to achieve in New Zealand. You have to entertain clubs from overseas before you get to the serious offer stage and I've never really gone past that. I've had a couple of very informal inquiries but I haven't really talked to anyone. I would look to do something overseas if I've contributed everything I can in New Zealand, but at this point I don't think I've done that."

It was a remarkable show of loyalty – especially as Mehrtens would soon have to front for Crusaders training with coach Robbie Deans. With Aaron Mauger, Daniel Carter and former NZ Colt Cameron McIntyre all vying for the two run-on spots at first and second-five the pressure was on for Mehrtens to arrive for the pre-season in something close to peak condition.

Mauger got the start for the first two Super 12 games of the campaign, loses against the Waratahs and Blues, before Mehrtens was brought back for the win against the Reds. The Crusaders got home 20-17 on the back of a try from Corey Flynn and five penalties from… Dan Carter. Mehrtens' role, even in victory, had been diminished. Talkback callers were convinced the treatment dished out from Deans to Mehrtens was personal.

"It's ludicrous, just a nonsense really," Deans told the *Dominion* of suggestions he and Mehrtens had fallen out. "I respect him hugely and I, probably more than anyone, want and have put time into assisting him to succeed. His international career has stalled but that doesn't mean to say it's ceased." Deans said Mehrtens had been out of favour in 2003 because he was unfit and out of form.

"He lost his ability to perform through his physical state last year, through injury and fitness." It meant Mehrtens could not run as he used to and Deans was wary of teams hanging off him and concentrating their defences on other players. "They call your bluff if you are not prepared to carry the ball."

Deans said he had been impressed by the work Mehrtens had done over summer to get himself fitter. "As a result of that his ability to perform is returning, his speed is coming back and with the experience he has he still offers a huge amount and is a hugely capable player. There is this hang up on game time. It's not about when and how much you play it's about what you do with it."

Someone with some insight in the relationship was Laurie Mains. The former All Blacks coach would often see Mehrtens around Queenstown – where they both owned property – and would run into Deans several times a season. His read on the relationship between the pair was simple. "At times Robbie found Andrew a bit testing in getting the commitment he wanted from him," Mains said. "Andrew had some stellar years under Robbie. When you have a long relationship inside a rugby team that is playing under pressure the whole time, you are going to have break downs in relationships. It's a matter of a fact. Stress and pressure will always create some disagreement. It's about how you work them out and come out the other end. And ultimately these two guys worked things out. I always sensed there was nothing but respect for each other between the two."

Mehrtens retained his position in the team after the scratchy win against the Reds and played in the wins against the Chiefs and Highlanders. Illness forced him out of the game against the Brumbies and when Cameron McIntyre led them to an impressive 47-28 win, life without Mehrtens looked bearable for some of the Crusaders' faithful.

Deans restored Mehrtens to the starting lineup for the game against the Sharks in Durban. And when the game was lost 25-29, Mehrtens paid the price. A furious Deans was unimpressed with his first five who had a clearance charged down early by Henno Mentz who scored, before a loose Mehrtens pass was scooped up by centre Adrian Jacobs who dashed 40m to score their second try. Deans said the Crusaders' performance was very poor. "It must be one of the ugliest performances I've witnessed. It's pretty disappointing from our perspective. We created our own problems, often we lacked composure on the ball and took poor options as a result. We gave up easy tries, we didn't force the Sharks to work for what they got and we weren't prepared to work. If we'd worked a little bit harder rather than forcing and trying to achieve in the first or second phase we would have got more out of the fixture."

Mehrtens didn't start a game for the Crusaders again in 2004. Deans, not even tempted to turn to his experience in the final in Canberra, until the Brumbies were so far in front that a stint from the bench was too little, too late for the franchise, player and coach. Mehrtens came on with the Crusaders trailing 33-0. He rallied the troops to give them a glimmer of hope. The Crusaders still lost 47-38 but Mehrtens had been crucial to the revival. "I guess it was really common sense," he said about coming on without any specific instructions

from the coach's box. "There were no real specific instructions other than that we had to find a way in, in terms of doing the job we were there for. The same thing was going through everyone's minds that you don't do anything fancy. You don't claw back a lead like that by throwing the ball around and doing something silly... just holding on to the ball and getting more guys to the breakdown. And they did tire out as the game went on so there were more and more gaps. We just had to hold on to the ball and use our knowledge of their game a wee bit better. We only needed to commit one or two guys to each ruck otherwise we had a massive underlap. It was just really simple rugby."

And, with everyone expecting him to bow his head for the last time and head for the first-class lounges with a one-way trip to a foreign club, he once again committed himself to a future in New Zealand. "The hunger is still there," he said. "I don't feel I'm done in New Zealand. I feel I've got more to offer and when I feel I don't, I'll look for another challenge. But my heart's still in New Zealand, my heart's still with Canterbury and the Crusaders. I'll just keep at it, think about the NPC and start working on that."

Graham Henry, now the All Blacks coach, selected Mehrtens in the All Blacks trial. And he put him on the Probable's bench – the shadow test team. Many were pleasantly shocked – including the player. "I was surprised (to be picked)," Mehrtens said. "It's been a difficult couple of years in that I haven't played well enough to warrant selection, week in, week out. Not being in that selection, I certainly didn't expect to be involved in the trials but I guess it's nice to get a message that you're still in the thoughts and still have something to offer. I really still have no expectations other than I just want to push myself and keep working on my game. It's almost like I have started again in the last year or so when I've had some more changes."

Mehrtens impressed in the trail, won by Tana Umaga's Probables side. Dan Carter got the headlines for slotting home a late penalty to secure a 29-27 win but it was Mehrtens who ignited a dormant Probables backline which scored two tries after his entrance for Carlos Spencer. Mehrtens also made a break that led to a Joe Rokocoko's try. It was an impressive performance and saw him win a place in the All Blacks squad for the home tests against England, Argentina and the Pacific Islands.

Which had people wondering, again, if Mehrtens felt hard done by Deans and the Crusaders. "At times I would have liked to have (played more) – it's tough because coaches and selectors have got to make a decision on whether they believe you can get a lot better. I guess if they're not seeing signs that they think you can during the week, or whatever, then they've got to judge based on that and they've got to make a decision for the best of the team. I was disappointed, I guess, not to be persisted with, but other guys took their chances at home and good luck to them. I've got no gripes at all."

And Deans told *Radio Sport* he was delighted at Mehrtens' All Blacks recall. "What people fail to understand is we are working together towards an end. We are not working against each other. I want to see him achieve, as much as I want to see any player achieve. I think it's fantastic he's been given an opportunity. He's shown he's got the zest for it, and I really hope it works out."

Mehrtens was very much the No 2 to Spencer in Graham Henry's All Blacks. And with Dan Carter set to star at second-five the problem that had dogged Spencer's international career – goal kicking – was now no longer an issue. So it was no surprise that Spencer played in both tests against an under-strength England

ABOVE: Graham Henry favoured Carlos Spencer in his early days as All Blacks coach.
PAGE 138: A good year for the Crusaders ensured Mehrtens would be back in black in 2004.
PAGE 141: Graham Henry never got the best out of Andrew Mehrtens.
PAGE 142: He was missing from the championship photo call but the Crusaders' wouldn't have won the Super 12 in 2000 without their inspirational first five.

side in Dunedin and Auckland. And with the tests won, it was clear that rotation was to be credited for Mehrtens' first test start against Wales in 2002 and when he was handed the No 10 jersey for the one-off test in Waikato against Argentina. Still, it was a moment that he said would be just as special as his debut in 1995.

"I just can't wait and am itching to step out there," said Mehrtens. "The thrill will be even better this time round. Even a little bit more so, because when I first got in the All Blacks it happened so quickly. Everything was new whereas having had the time off last year I knew what it meant to me. You can't cherish it until you've got it and I really cherish it a lot more this time." Mehrtens said he was floored when told he'd got the start. "I think I'm getting better, more to a position where I can contribute to more areas of the game. In the past, the way the game was you could sit back a little bit more at first five and rely on a kicking game and run every now and then. For a while I didn't adapt as quickly to the modern game as other players did so I am trying to catch up to that now."

Doug Golightly, *The Truth*'s sport editor was, like most of the rugby nation, thrilled. "If you like rugby success stories, look at Andrew Mehrtens. He's been named to start this weekend's test match against Argentina and it's difficult to sidestep the fact that his is one of the most inspiring rugby yarns of recent times. And the reason? Well, it seemed the Canterbury pivot's career had been consigned to the history books. The critics said he was washed up and he was sidelined by former All Blacks coach John Mitchell and his Crusaders boss Robbie Deans. Opportunities for Mehrtens to show what he's capable of were fast disappearing. In fact, many fans and commentators speculated that he'd never be back. How wrong they were. Spurred on by a hard work ethic, an intense competitive desire to succeed and a new relationship, Mehrtens has emerged once again as a reliable match winner. It's something he can be proud of."

Mehrtens' performance in the 41-7 win against Argentina wasn't one of his best in the black jersey. But that was insignificant to most on that night. The night was about the comeback. How he had looked adversity in the eye and beaten it. A win for David against Goliath. Graham Henry though, emotionless as he had to be, decided that the few errors Mehrtens came up with in Hamilton were enough to keep him out of the test squad for the Pacific Islanders test. Nick Evans, the Otago utility, would provide the back up to Spencer (first five) and Dan Carter (goal kicking).

With the Islanders dispatched 41-26 it was time for the Tri-nations. Mehrtens was sent back to Christchurch to play some club rugby. And while the All Blacks beat Australia 16-7 in Wellington before scrapping home 23-21 against the 'Boks at Jade Stadium, there were concerns about Carlos Spencer's ability to control a test match.

Spencer was looking over his shoulder as the All Blacks prepared for the return game against the Wallabies in Sydney after Mehrtens was named in the All Blacks reserves. "One of the selectors (Steve Hansen) watched Andrew in the club final in Christchurch and he was outstanding," Graham Henry said. "And there is every chance he will get some game time off the bench."

The All Blacks crashed to their first defeat under Henry at Telstra Stadium losing 23-18. Spencer's liabilities at the highest level had been shown up once again. Chris Mirams, writing in the *Sunday Star Times* didn't hold back. "Andrew Mehrtens," he wrote, "replaced Spencer in the 51st minute after the Aucklander's game deteriorated to the point he was as comfortable as a rabbi served a pork chop."

Henry named Mehrtens in the line-up to play the final Tri-nations game, against South Africa in Johannesburg. With Sam Tuitupou in for the injured Dan Carter, Mehrtens was also handed the kicking responsibilities. And while all looked rosy for Mehrtens from the outside looking in, a conversation with Laurie

Mains the day before the test suggests otherwise. Henry – a strict coach by any definition – is not big on players expressing themselves. And in this test, which would be Mehrtens' last, he was under strict instructions. It was his 70th test but he wasn't being left to think on his feet. His kicked his goals – two conversions and four penalties – but the game would be lost 40-26.

"I believe I understand Andrew pretty well," Mains said in 2007. "You could be right upfront with Andrew. If there was something he didn't do right or didn't do according to instructions, you could tell him straight up and it would have no negative effect provided you then went to the positives and kept him in a very positive frame of mind. I believe that when he had lapses of his best form it was simply because he wasn't being handled the right way mentally. I saw him not doing things at times that were bread and butter for him. With Andrew it was always the case that you would get the best out of him if you showed him that you believed in him and you gave him a clear game plan that he was to play too.

"What team management have to do is invest in players and get the best out of them by handling them the best way possible. We don't always do that – I know I didn't always do it – but Andrew was one who I had the measure of and I knew how to get the best out of him. I ran into him and Justin Marshall at a golf course in Johannesburg before that Tri-nations game in 2004. We were talking about the game the next day and I said 'Listen Andrew, you know the rules about playing at altitude, don't you? You've got to get field position…' And this cheeky little grin came across his face. Andrew? He said 'I've got to do what I'm told – not what I necessarily think is best.' After we left them, I said to the boys I was with, 'They will play the wrong game tomorrow.' Sure enough, they lost.

"Andrew used to express an opinion to me if he thought the game plan wasn't right. But here was an example nine years later of not expressing an opinion to his current coach. And I found that astoundingly sad. I think he needed coaches that believed in him and gave him a game plan that he was happy with.

"Graham Henry should have recognized Andrew's intelligence needed to be respected. If you discussed what you needed to get out of him for the team to win, and it was a two way discussion, he'd be totally happy and he'd go out there and do what you agreed he would do. I don't think he was ever the sort of player that you would dictate too. You can do that with some players but not with Andrew. He is a very intelligent, knowledgeable rugby player. There would be very few coaches that know more about the game than him."

ANDREW Mehrtens is still searching… Searching for the perfect game. Now, into the first year of his time at French second division outfit Toulon, it's almost an obsession. But can we blame him? What else is there to play for? A perfect ending? He'd already had that.

HIS last full season with Canterbury had ended in 2004 with the NPC championship and the knowledge that in his 100th game for his province he'd kicked 18 points against Bay of Plenty – a win that saw the Ranfurly Shield returned to the Canterbury Rugby Union's trophy cabinet. In one of his 11 appearances for the Crusaders in 2005 he overtook Matthew Burke as the competition's record point's scorer when he landed a 35m penalty against the Cats. And then, in the winning final against the Waratahs, Robbie Deans brought Mehrtens on late in the game so the Jade Stadium faithful could honour their favourite son one last time.

Soon after, and now 32, he was joining the famed London club Harlequins on a two-year deal. The statistical highlights of his career in New Zealand were his 967 points in tests, a record for the All Blacks and

the third highest in the world behind Welshman Neil Jenkins and Argentina's Diego Dominguez. His 167 test conversions were a world record, while his 209 points against South Africa was the highest achieved by any player against any country and his 202 against Australia was the second highest.

The tributes flowed. Graham Henry: "Andrew has been a world-class player and was probably the best No 10 in the world in the late 1990s, over the last decade he has been one of our foremost All Blacks and a great character."

Teammate Aaron Mauger: "He's been probably one of the greatest players New Zealand's ever had I suppose and he's contributed a lot to All Black rugby and to Canterbury rugby and he's been a good mate to all of us so it's certainly sad to see him go, Mehrts being the person that he is and what he'd achieved is always going to be something special and something to aspire to for any young fella."

Canterbury coach Aussie McLean: "Like the great Michael Jordan, if Mehrts was in your team you had a pretty good chance of winning it. For as many as six years he has been critical to the winning and losing of games. Off the field he is also a fantastic talisman for Canterbury rugby."

But New Zealand rugby was losing more than a great All Black. We were losing a great character. And Mehrtens reassured his public that this was the right move at the right time. "I'm really looking forward to playing for one team throughout the whole season. It's been tough going through 10 years of the Crusaders, All Blacks and Canterbury all with different regimes, and people rightly expect you to peak for each one, week in and out. I like the thought of planning out one whole season with one team and knowing when the breaks are rather than going into the New Zealand season with a reasonable amount of uncertainty. A number of things about the move appealed to me including the lifestyle thing. There are a lot of peripheral things in rugby that I don't enjoy.

"I chose Harlequins because I liked the feel of their club ... a good history, steeped in tradition. I do want a challenge in rugby. My contribution has dwindled in teams I've been in the last few years with a lot of younger players coming through who are faster and stronger. But I still love the opportunity to get in and play week in and out."

Mehrtens said he would also relish not living in the public eye which saw the high profile first five-eighths make news off the field when he lost form. "I am looking forward to being in a new environment and not anticipating being under the spotlight. I'll hide myself away and it depends what the media is like at Exeter and Rotherham who Harlequins will be lining up against next season. I'm not saying I've had a bad run here, there have been people who had a lot worse dealt out to them from the media. I don't want to sound uncharitable. It's just I think these days the rugby scene is a lot different to 10 years ago. There's so much more attention it's a lot harder to get away from rugby. It's part of it, I guess, and guys coming in as youngsters nowadays are more used to it. I don't want to sound nothing's the way it used to be. We are competing for the entertainment dollar and there's some aspects of it I don't like. Being judged by people who I feel have no knowledge of rugby and in many cases have no knowledge of sport has been pretty annoying. Being in a team game where you are relying on your mates to help you out and you're trying to help your mates out with the way you do things and the way they do things – then to be judged individually a lot is pretty annoying and shows again a reasonable lack of understanding of the game as well so that's been pretty frustrating. But I guess you get that everywhere and shows the interest New Zealanders have for rugby. Everyone's got good and bad aspects to their job. There are lots of fantastic things I will miss hugely but some things I won't but I guess that's natural."

There was one more game to be played on New Zealand soil – for his beloved Canterbury in a Ranfurly Shield defence against Marlborough. "Mehrts is the greatest player we've (Canterbury) ever had," said Aussie McLean. "He's dominated New Zealand rugby for close to a decade. It's very rare in a team game like rugby to have one individual who when he runs out there he makes such a difference to the result and that's what makes him so special."

And with that, Mehrtens was gone to lead Harlequins to promotion in his first year before signing on to join Tana Umaga at Toulon along with an all-star cast which also included the great Australian halfback George Gregan and South Africa's lineout colossus Victor Matfield. "That's quite fitting isn't," Laurie Mains said. "He deserves to be surrounded by some of the great names in rugby from this modern era as he bows out of the game. He deserves it because he is one of the greats – even if certain coaches struggled to see the genius in him..."

MEHRTS: THE ALL BLACK

FULL NAME	Andrew Philip Mehrtens
BORN	Saturday, 28 April 1973 in Durban
AGE	34
PHYSICAL	1.78m, 89kg
POSITION	First five-eighth
LAST SCHOOL	Christchurch Boys' High
RUGBY CLUB	
(First made All Blacks from)	Christchurch HSOB
PROVINCE	Canterbury
SUPER 14 TEAM	Crusaders
ALL BLACK DEBUT	Saturday, 22 April 1995
	v Canada at Auckland
	aged 21 years, 359 days
INTERNATIONAL DEBUT	Saturday, 22 April 1995
	v Canada at Auckland
	aged 21 years, 359 days
LAST TEST	Saturday, 14 August 2004
	v South Africa at Johannesburg
	aged 31 years, 108 days
ALL BLACK TESTS	70
ALL BLACK GAMES	2
TOTAL ALL BLACK MATCHES	72
ALL BLACK TEST POINTS	967pts (7t, 169c, 188p, 10dg)
ALL BLACK GAME POINTS	27pts (0t, 3c, 7p, 0dg)
TOTAL ALL BLACK POINTS	994pts (7t, 172c, 195p, 10dg)
ALL BLACK NUMBER	944

ALL BLACK GAMES

Statistics courtesy of the New Zealand Rugby Museum

1995
22 Apr	vs **Canada** at Auckland 73-7
27 May	vs **Ireland** at Johannesburg 43-19
31 May	vs **Wales** at Johannesburg 34-9
11 Jun	vs **Scotland** at Pretoria 48-30
18 Jun	vs **England** at Cape Town 45-29
24 Jun	vs **South Africa** at Johannesburg 12-15
22 Jul	vs **Australia** at Auckland 28-16
29 Jul	vs **Australia** at Sydney 34-23
25 Oct	vs **Italy 'A'** at Catania 51-21 (-)

1996
7 Jun	vs **Samoa** at Napier 51-10
15 Jun	vs **Scotland** at Dunedin 62-31
22 Jun	vs **Scotland** at Auckland 36-12
6 Jul	vs **Australia** at Wellington 43-6
20 Jul	vs **South Africa** at Christchurch 15-11
27 Jul	vs **Australia** at Brisbane 32-25
10 Aug	vs **South Africa** at Cape Town 29-18
31 Aug	vs **South Africa** at Johannesburg 22-32

1997
14 Jun	vs **Fiji** at Albany 71-5 (-)
9 Aug	vs **South Africa** at Auckland 55-35 (+)
8 Nov	vs **Llanelli** at Llanelli 81-3 (-)
15 Nov	vs **Ireland** at Dublin 63-15 (-)
22 Nov	vs **England** at Manchester 25-8
29 Nov	vs **Wales** at London 42-7
6 Dec	vs **England** at London 26-26

1998
20 Jun	vs **England** at Dunedin 64-22
27 Jun	vs **England** at Auckland 40-10
11 Jul	vs **Australia** at Melbourne 16-24 (-)
25 Jul	vs **South Africa** at Wellington 3-13 (+)
1 Aug	vs **Australia** at Christchurch 23-27
15 Aug	vs **South Africa** at Durban 23-24
29 Aug	vs **Australia** at Sydney 14-19 (-)

1999
26 Jun	vs **France** at Wellington 54-7 (-)
10 Jul	vs **South Africa** at Dunedin 28-0 (-)
24 Jul	vs **Australia** at Auckland 34-15 (-)
7 Aug	vs **South Africa** at Pretoria 34-18
28 Aug	vs **Australia** at Sydney 7-28 (-)
3 Oct	vs **Tonga** at Bristol 45-9
9 Oct	vs **England** at London 30-16 (-)
24 Oct	vs **Scotland** at Edinburgh 30-18 (-)
31 Oct	vs **France** at London 31-43
4 Nov	vs **South Africa** at Cardiff 18-22

2000
24 Jun	vs **Scotland** at Dunedin 69-20
1 Jul	vs **Scotland** at Auckland 48-14 (-)
15 Jul	vs **Australia** at Sydney 39-35 (-)
22 Jul	vs **South Africa** at Christchurch 25-12 (-)
5 Aug	vs **Australia** at Wellington 23-24 (-)
19 Aug	vs **South Africa** at Johannesburg 40-46
11 Nov	vs **France** at Paris 39-26
18 Nov	vs **France** at Marseille 33-42
25 Nov	vs **Italy** at Genova 56-19 (+)

2001
23 Jun	vs **Argentina** at Christchurch 67-19 (-)
11 Aug	vs **Australia** at Dunedin 15-23 (+)
25 Aug	vs **South Africa** at Auckland 26-15
1 Sep	vs **Australia** at Sydney 26-29
17 Nov	vs **Ireland** at Dublin 40-29
24 Nov	vs **Scotland** at Edinburgh 37-6
1 Dec	vs **Argentina** at Buenos Aires 24-20

2002
8 Jun	vs **Italy** at Hamilton 64-10
15 Jun	vs **Ireland** at Dunedin 15-6
22 Jun	vs **Ireland** at Auckland 40-8
29 Jun	vs **Fiji** at Wellington 68-18 (+)(-)
13 Jul	vs **Australia** at Christchurch 12-6
20 Jul	vs **South Africa** at Wellington 41-20
3 Aug	vs **Australia** at Sydney 14-16 (-)
10 Aug	vs **South Africa** at Durban 30-23
9 Nov	vs **England** at London 28-31 (+)
16 Nov	vs **France** at Paris 20-20
23 Nov	vs **Wales** at Cardiff 43-17

2004
19 Jun	vs **England** at Auckland 36-12 (+)
26 Jun	vs **Argentina** at Hamilton 41-7
7 Aug	vs **Australia** at Sydney 18-23 (+)
14 Aug	vs **South Africa** at Johannesburg 26-40

(+) = substitute
(-) = replaced

POINTS SCORED FOR THE ALL BLACKS

	t	c	p	dg	pts
vs Canada, 22 Apr 1995	1	7	3	-	28
vs Ireland, 27 May 1995	-	3	4	-	18
vs Wales, 31 May 1995	-	2	4	1	19
vs Scotland, 11 Jun 1995	1	6	2	-	23
vs England, 18 Jun 1995	-	3	1	1	12
vs South Africa, 24 Jun 1995	-	-	3	1	12
vs Australia, 22 Jul 1995	-	1	5	2	23
vs Australia, 29 Jul 1995	1	3	1	-	14
vs Italy 'A', 25 Oct 1995	-	1	5	-	17
vs Samoa, 7 Jun 1996	-	5	1	1	16
vs Scotland, 15 Jun 1996	1	7	1	-	22
vs Scotland, 22 Jun 1996	-	4	1	-	11
vs Australia, 6 Jul 1996	-	2	3	-	13
vs South Africa, 20 Jul 1996	-	-	5	-	15
vs Australia, 27 Jul 1996	-	2	6	-	22
vs South Africa, 10 Aug 1996	-	2	5	-	19
vs South Africa, 31 Aug 1996	-	2	1	-	7
vs Fiji, 14 Jun 1997	-	6	-	-	12
vs Llanelli, 8 Nov 1997	-	2	2	-	10
vs Ireland, 15 Nov 1997	1	5	6	-	33
vs England, 22 Nov 1997	-	2	2	-	10
vs Wales, 29 Nov 1997	-	4	2	-	14
vs England, 6 Dec 1997	1	2	4	-	21
vs England, 20 Jun 1998	-	5	3	-	19
vs England, 27 Jun 1998	-	2	-	-	4
vs Australia, 11 Jul 1998	-	-	1	-	3
vs South Africa, 25 Jul 1998	-	-	1	-	3
vs Australia, 1 Aug 1998	-	2	3	-	13
vs South Africa, 15 Aug 1998	-	2	3	-	13
vs Australia, 29 Aug 1998	-	-	2	1	9
vs France, 26 Jun 1999	-	5	3	-	19
vs South Africa, 10 Jul 1999	-	1	3	-	11
vs Australia, 24 Jul 1999	-	1	9	-	29
vs South Africa, 7 Aug 1999	-	-	7	-	21
vs Australia, 28 Aug 1999	1	1	-	-	7
vs Tonga, 3 Oct 1999	-	4	4	-	20
vs England, 9 Oct 1999	-	3	3	-	15
vs Scotland, 24 Oct 1999	-	2	2	-	10
vs France, 31 Oct 1999	-	2	4	-	16
vs South Africa, 4 Nov 1999	-	-	6	-	18
vs Scotland, 24 Jun 2000	-	7	-	-	14
vs Scotland, 1 Jul 2000	-	3	-	-	6
vs Australia, 15 Jul 2000	-	4	2	-	14
vs South Africa, 22 Jul 2000	-	-	3	1	12
vs Australia, 5 Aug 2000	-	2	3	-	13
vs South Africa, 19 Aug 2000	-	4	3	1	20
vs France, 11 Nov 2000	-	1	9	-	29

	t	c	p	dg	pts
vs France, 18 Nov 2000	-	3	4	-	18
vs Argentina, 23 Jun 2001	-	3	1	-	9
vs Australia, 11 Aug 2001	-	1	-	-	2
vs South Africa, 25 Aug 2001	-	2	4	-	16
vs Australia, 1 Sep 2001	-	2	4	-	16
vs Ireland, 17 Nov 2001	-	5	-	-	10
vs Scotland, 24 Nov 2001	-	2	6	-	22
vs Argentina, 1 Dec 2001	-	1	4	-	14
vs Italy, 8 Jun 2002	-	8	1	-	19
vs Ireland, 15 Jun 2002	-	1	1	-	5
vs Ireland, 22 Jun 2002	-	3	3	-	15
vs Australia, 13 Jul 2002	-	-	4	-	12
vs South Africa, 20 Jul 2002	-	2	3	1	16
vs Australia, 3 Aug 2002	-	-	3	-	9
vs South Africa, 10 Aug 2002	-	2	2	-	10
vs England, 9 Nov 2002	-	2	-	-	4
vs France, 16 Nov 2002	-	2	2	-	10
vs Wales, 23 Nov 2002	-	4	5	-	23
vs Argentina, 26 Jun 2004	-	5	2	-	16
vs Australia, 7 Aug 2004	-	-	1	-	3
vs South Africa, 14 Aug 2004	-	2	4	-	16
Totals	**7**	**172**	**195**	**10**	**994**

TEST RECORD BY NATION

	P	W	D	L	t	c	p	dg	pts
Argentina	3	3	-	-	-	9	7	-	39
Australia	16	7	-	9	2	21	47	3	202
Canada	1	1	-	-	1	7	3	-	28
England	8	6	1	1	1	19	13	1	85
Fiji	2	2	-	-	-	6	-	-	12
France	5	2	1	2	-	13	22	-	92
Ireland	5	5	-	-	1	17	14	-	81
Italy	2	2	-	-	-	8	1	-	19
Samoa	1	1	-	-	-	5	1	1	16
Scotland	7	7	-	-	2	31	12	-	108
South Africa	16	9	-	7	-	19	53	4	209
Tonga	1	1	-	-	-	4	4	-	20
Wales	3	3	-	-	-	10	11	1	56
TOTALS	**70**	**49**	**2**	**19**	**7**	**169**	**188**	**10**	**967**

ABOUT THE AUTHOR

This is John Matheson's ninth book. In 1999 he collaborated with Eric Rush on the best seller *Gold Rush* and in 2000 he penned the critically acclaimed *Black Days* – a series of interviews with rugby superstars recounting their experiences of playing against the All Blacks. In 2002 there was another No 1 best seller - *Rushie*, the second book with Rush and a biography on league star Stacey Jones. They were followed by *Life on the Run* the best selling biography on All Blacks great Christian Cullen – the third biggest selling rugby book in New Zealand.

In 2004 he completed the Rush trilogy when he wrote, *Adrenalin Rush*. And last year he wrote *Tana Umaga – A Tribute to a Rugby Legend*, a celebration of the 2005 Grand Slam winning captain's career as well as the critically acclaimed *All Whites '82* – the inside story of New Zealand soccer's greatest World Cup campaign.

Throughout his 21 years in journalism he has worked in Auckland, Christchurch, London and San Diego and has covered such diverse sporting events as the Rugby World Cup, Grand Slam tennis, World Cup soccer, the NBA and the America's Cup.

While in New Zealand he has worked for the *Auckland Star* and *Sunday Star*, contributed to the *New Zealand Herald* and the *Dominion*, is still the longest serving editor of *NZ Rugby World*. He is currently an Assistant Editor and Sports Editor at *Sunday News*.

Matheson – a five-time recipient at the Qantas Media Awards and a eight-time finalist at the National Sports Journalism Awards – directed the Sky TV rugby show *Offside* and lists completing the Ironman, playing for and coaching Auckland basketball teams and being offered a trial by Harry Redknapp at Bournemouth as three of his proudest achievements.

He wishes to thank HarperCollins' Bill Honeybone for his continued support.

Matheson dedicates his part in this book to his guiding light, daughter Ava-Dawn May Matheson, born on February 3, 2006 and partner Jessica May Galu.

ISBN (13-digit): 978 1 86950 697 1
ISBN (10-digit): 1 86950 697 9

Published in 2007 by
HarperCollins*Publishers (New Zealand) Limited*
P.O. Box 1, Auckland
New Zealand

Cover design: Dexter Fry
Book design and production: Gina Hochstein
Printed in China by Prolong Press, Hong Kong

10 9 8 7 6 5 4 3 2 1

Whilst every effort has been made to correctly acknowledge the contributors to this book, the publishers cannot be held responsible for any errors or omissions. Incorrect attributions that are brought to their attention will be corrected in future printings.

The photographs used on the cover are supplied by Jo Caird

THE PHOTOGRAPHS
Jo Caird:
pages 2, 4, 7, 10–11, 12, 19, 25, 30–31, 32, 35, 39, 42, 44, 47, 58, 59, 60, 64, 68, 72, 74, 77, 78, 81, 82, 85, 92, 95, 96–97, 98, 99, 102, 105, 106–107, 112, 116, 118–119, 124, 132–133, 134, 138, 142–143, 146–147
TRANZ/POPPERFOTO:
pages 8, 16, 20, 28, 55, 67, 144
TRANZ/Reuters:
pages 15, 22-23, 25, 36–37, 41, 48–49, 52, 56, 63, 71, 86, 89, 90–91, 100, 108, 110, 111,115, 120–121, 123, 127, 128,129, 131, 137, 141
TRANZ/Corbis:
page 50